THE
FIRST LADIES

FROM MARTHA WASHINGTON
TO MAMIE EISENHOWER,
AN INTIMATE PORTRAIT
OF THE WOMEN
WHO SHAPED AMERICA

FEATHER
SCHWARTZ FOSTER

CUMBERLAND HOUSE™

Copyright © 2011 by Feather Schwartz Foster
Cover and internal design © 2011 by Sourcebooks, Inc.
Cover design by Roy Roper/wideyedesign
Cover images © wynnter/iStockphoto.com; Bettmann/CORBIS
All images of First Ladies are courtesy of the Library of Congress.

Sourcebooks and the colophon are registered trademarks of Sourcebooks, Inc.

Published by Cumberland House, an imprint of Sourcebooks, Inc.
P.O. Box 4410, Naperville, Illinois 60567–4410
(630) 961–3900
Fax: (630) 961–2168
www.sourcebooks.com

Library of Congress Cataloging-in-Publication Data

Schwartz Foster, Feather.
  The first ladies : From Martha Washington to Mamie Eisenhower, an intimate portrait of the women who shaped America / Feather Schwartz Foster.
      p. cm.
  Includes bibliographical references.

  1. Presidents' spouses—United States—Biography. I. Title.

E176.2.S37 2011
973.09'9—dc22
  [B]
                              2010041948

Printed and bound in the United States of America.
VP 10 9 8 7 6 5 4 3 2 1

To the Ladies themselves…

TABLE OF CONTENTS

ACKNOWLEDGMENTS

To the docents of the dozens of presidential sites I have visited over the years, who have cheerfully put up with my zillion questions.

My personal presidential library full of nearly two thousand volumes—far too many to list. Their authors taught me to read and write. And think.

The staff of the Scotch Plains, New Jersey, library, where I was a fixture for years, scribbling away.

The staff of the Williamsburg, Virginia, library, where I am currently a fixture and plan to continue to be for years to come.

To the editors at Sourcebooks, who have been patient with me and more helpful than they realize.

To Dr. Paul C. Nagel, who encouraged me and helped more than he could ever know.

To Ron Pitkin, who believed in me.

To the memory of Laura G. Haywood, who put me on the path and kept after me.

To my dear friend Barbara Lepis, who instinctively asks the right questions.

And finally, to my husband and daughter, who have been sharing me with a bunch of old gals for a very long time.

MARTHA WASHINGTON
1731–1802

FIRST LADY: 1789–97

The Domestic Lady W.

It has been said that the best political decision George Washington ever made was to marry the Widow Custis. He was a Virginia militia colonel seeking a career change. Efforts for a commission in the regular British army had been consistently thwarted. Washington determined to focus his attentions on the estate he had inherited from his half brother, but in order to make his Mount Vernon plantation the envy of Fairfax County, he needed an appropriate consort. And it was time. He was twenty-six.

Martha Dandridge Custis was the daughter of well-to-do

Virginia gentry on a social and economic par with the Washingtons. Her academic education was modest. She could read, write, and do sufficient arithmetic to manage the household accounts. At seventeen, she married into the wealthy Custis family and was widowed at twenty-six, left with two small children (four and two years old), and one huge estate (more than twenty thousand fertile acres, two hundred slaves, and the scarcest commodity among land-poor planters: a substantial amount of cash). Remarriage was her best option, and Martha required a mate with sufficient property of his own, since she was understandably wary of fortune hunters. She also required someone who would be a kind stepfather and honest manager for her children's sizable inheritance.

Both of them made fortunate choices for a happy and successful marriage.

Martha was the consummate colonial mistress and hostess, reasonably cultured, and superbly skilled at household management. It would fall to her to supervise the numerous slaves and cottage industries that accounted for a successful plantation. She sewed beautifully, danced the minuet gracefully, was said to set the finest table in northern Virginia. Her kitchen and recipe collection was the envy of her neighbors. She boasted a medical box with all the proper herbs and remedies the eighteenth century could provide, and she took pride and pleasure in caring for others.

The Custis wealth helped to assure Washington a seat in the House of Burgesses, a responsibility he accepted with the usual eighteenth-century noblesse oblige. Within ten years of their marriage, Washington had increased his own holdings to include acreage as far west as the Ohio Valley. Mount Vernon had been renovated and enlarged. Most important, he had established and engaged more than a dozen tenant farmers and craftsmen to provide mills, shipbuilding facilities, a fishing fleet, spinners, and weavers for his ever-growing conglomerate of industries. The Washingtons had become extremely wealthy, thanks to his shrewd business instincts, but they seldom dined alone. Their home was a mecca for friends and neighbors, relations on both sides, and weary travelers. No one was turned away. Their hospitality was known throughout the colony.

Martha's Legacy

Everything Martha Washington did between 1789 and 1797 set a precedent and **TONE** for future First Ladies determined by her modest gentility and coupled with years of executive skills at plantation-house management. The exquisitely fine line walked between a dreaded monarchy à la England and the rabble of democracy à la France would find no finer example than that of Lady Washington. Her elegance was simple. Her natural friendliness seeped through the prescribed deportment. The tone she set was completely new. And it was decidedly American.

At the onset of the American Revolution, both George and Martha were forty-three, which was considered well into middle age. War in the eighteenth century was primarily a seasonal affair: spring, summer, and fall. In the winter, armies usually went into winter quarters, and Martha Washington would travel from Mount Vernon with her medicine box and knitting needles to meet her husband wherever he was encamped. She had never before ventured beyond Virginia's borders. The exacting general, who was always hard-pressed to maintain his ragtag army, heartily welcomed Mrs. W. and whatever supplies she could bring, which were a godsend. She immediately took charge of seeing to the general's personal comfort, supervising the officers' kitchens, and organizing other officers' wives to sew, knit, scrape lint for bandages, and make themselves useful. Above all, she had her medicine box for tending the sick and wounded. Come spring, she went home and the war continued.

It would be seven years before Private Citizen and Mrs. Washington could be together again in their beloved Virginia home. Their idyll would not last long. Politics would take center stage in the new nation, and Washington was considered the indispensable man with a new title: president of the United States. There had never been anything like it before.

How would he and Lady Washington behave in this new office? It was virgin territory. Every known political paradigm was based on royalty or quasi royalty, and this had been so for nearly two thousand years. There was no precedent for a republic on the scale of the tiny United States on the vast continent of America. How would they chart the course for generations to come?

Lady W. (some honorific was needed, and aristocratic titles were verboten) was nearly sixty and not about to change her ways—certainly not willingly. She continued to dress in the same simple fashions she had worn for decades and determined to remain refined and dignified. But she had a serious predicament. Her elevation in social stature as the premier woman in the country precluded her traditional Virginia hospitality. She could not appear aloof and remote, since it would smack of monarchial tendencies. But neither could she be warm and welcoming, as was her nature. It would suggest an unbecoming familiarity for a head of state. After a lifetime of full houses and of exchanging frequent visits with friends and family, the new protocol made her feel isolated. Some middle ground had to be met. But how?

She was happy, of course, to open the presidential home in New York and later in Philadelphia (rented in both cases) for entertaining. Political dinners for President Washington were usually stag affairs. Martha would plan and supervise, but she did not attend. Instead, she instituted regular drawing room levees, inviting carefully selected guests for carefully prepared entertainments, trying to tiptoe that fine line required for a republican court. People were contemptuous of royal trappings, but they definitely wanted some glitz. Martha was decorous but not glitzy. Obviously she could not please everyone. The criticism in society, in the political world, and in the press annoyed her.

Having tirelessly devoted themselves to the welfare of their country, valuing honorable conduct above all else, both Washingtons were notably thin-skinned and sensitive to public reproach for their behavior, which they believed to be estimable at all times. Martha resented being watched by the colonial paparazzi and criticized at every turn. Where did she go? What did she wear? Whom did she speak to? Which carriage did she use? Why did she sit on a slightly raised platform at her receptions? What did all this mean? It rankled her to no end, so she chose to go out as seldom as possible, pining for the time she could return to Mount Vernon and their own vine and fig tree.

It was a difficult line to walk, and both Washingtons were more than happy to finally relinquish the power, the glory, and the comments. For the first time in twenty years, they could sit down to dinner by themselves.

Postscript: DESPITE PETTY COLONIAL-STYLE GOSSIP, MARTHA WASHINGTON HAS GONE DOWN IN HISTORY SIMILARLY TO HER ILLUSTRIOUS HUSBAND: ABOVE REPROACH AND REMEMBERED FOR ESTABLISHING A NEARLY IMPOSSIBLE POSITION.

ABIGAIL ADAMS
1744–1818

FIRST LADY: 1797–1801

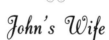

John's Wife

Even if John Adams's immortality had been only as a signer of the Declaration of Independence, his wife would still be considered the preeminent colonial woman. For all the intellectual brilliance and wisdom of Abigail Smith Adams, her contribution strictly as First Lady is adequate but certainly not outstanding. Her huge contribution to history is purely as John's wife. And what a wife she was!

John Adams met the fourteen-year-old minister's daughter in her own house. At twenty-three, the young lawyer occasionally stayed with the Smith family when he was in

Weymouth, Massachusetts, attending to legal business. The young girl's wit, outspoken manner, and pithy questions attracted him from the start, and they began courting in earnest when she was seventeen. They married a month before her twentieth birthday.

Abigail's Legacy

Not so much as First Lady but by being herself and being John's wife, Abigail Adams brought **SCOPE** to the role of First Lady. Only a rare few mistresses of the White House have embodied the wisdom, insight, political savvy, and acumen to make them not only their husband's partner but a genuine confidante and advisor. Barely known to most of her countrymen during her lifetime, once her correspondence was published a quarter century after her death, Abigail became a beacon and example of some of the finest attributes to which any woman could aspire. Today she ranks high in that pantheon where intelligence and wisdom is an admired attribute.

The Adams marriage was a remarkable partnership for their times. Abigail once said that their hearts were "cast in the same mold." She possessed all the usual domestic skills of a New England housewife, but while Abigail was homeschooled, she was well educated, particularly in unladylike subjects such as philosophy, theology, economics, and politics. John encouraged her serious interests. Had he not, had he relegated her to the customary domesticity of eighteenth-century womanly behavior, Abigail Adams would likely have provided nothing more than a series of almanac facts for historians. As it was, however, she buoyed him when he was in one of his despairs, soothed his recurrent spells of crankiness, and never failed to encourage his best efforts. He in turn was that rare man who appreciated a good mind wherever he found it, and if it was in the body of a woman—even his wife—so be it. He sincerely valued her prescient and insightful opinions and willingly gave her the respect and esteem she well deserved. Abigail had always enjoyed the abstract concept of politics and understood it as well as any male contemporary.

By the time she was thirty, Abigail was raising four small children in a tiny saltbox house, maintaining their modest farm, and devoting herself to running the household with limited funds and only seasonal or day help. They were never a wealthy family, and Abigail did her own housework, cooking, and sewing. She doctored the children when they were sick. She tutored all four in their basics until they were ready for neighborhood schooling. She maintained regular social contact within her community. And she did it alone. Her husband was four hundred miles away in Philadelphia, trying to form a new nation.

John delighted in their lively correspondence wherein they discussed all the events of the day, the potentials for unknown tomorrows, plus insights into the complex personalities that made up the Continental Congress. Their letters, a treasure trove for history, are peppered with lively comments, sprightly exchanges, genuine respect and counsel, and overwhelming encouragement and affection for each other.

After nearly a decade of long separations, John finally sent for her. By the mid-1780s he had been dispatched to Europe to chart treaties for America's peace and trade. "Come to Paris," he said. Nearly forty, Abigail had never ventured farther than Boston. Everything she knew about France, including the language, was from books. She was totally unprepared for her great awakening. Like most Puritan-reared New Englanders, she came to Europe with a lifetime of prejudices: European society was decadent, scandalous, expensive, sacrilegious, and shocking to her preconceived moral values. What she learned, however, was that other values might have merit and that she could be open to change.

The ballet, for instance, which she found immoral at first, with women wearing flesh-colored tights and short skirts, became beautiful and graceful once she became exposed to it. The social liberties granted to women astonished and then delighted her. Her ingrained republican (small "r") standards and principles would also moderate in Europe, as she began to appreciate some of the benefits of societal order, hierarchy, and etiquette. She learned that the elegant trappings of the Old World had a definite place, even in the coarse and rugged New World across the Atlantic.

When John and Abigail returned to their beloved New England, duty again called, this time to New York and then

Philadelphia. John Adams had been elected vice president of the new United States. Abigail was in residence only sporadically, however. Her health, never robust, was becoming iffier. Their new house in Braintree, purchased by proxy when they were still abroad, needed remodeling and supervision. Two of their children were not prospering, and it would eventually fall to Abigail to raise several grandchildren. Most of all, John hated his job, calling it "the most insignificant office ever devised by the hand of man." He would escape back to Massachusetts at every opportunity. Nevertheless, when Abigail *was* available to fulfill her role as Second Lady, she performed graciously and in a spirit of friendship with Lady Washington. The two women sincerely liked each other.

Mrs. Adams was well known in political circles by the time she reached New York, at least by reputation. Her husband had spoken of her often over the years, and Abigail had engaged in her own personal correspondence with many notables of the day. (While conversation between the sexes was severely curtailed in the eighteenth century, written communication was permitted.) All were aware of her fine mind, as well as her noticeable lack of restraint in expressing herself. John, no shrinking violet himself, cautioned her that "we must both hold our tongues." For her part, she grumbled about imposing "a silence upon myself, when I long to talk."

Abigail did not attend her husband's inauguration as president. She was nursing Old Mrs. Adams Senior, who would die within weeks. Abigail at fifty-four was also suffering from one of her frequent agues. Her nonprospering children were now actively failing (with the exception of John Quincy), and she was pulled in many directions at once. But John needed her too, and she never failed him. He needed her counsel; he needed to talk things out with her. She was the perfect sounding board; he called her "his best and wisest advisor." She was also needed to furnish and manage the president's house in Philadelphia—an expense that rankled her. But she came often and stayed as long as possible, bringing wagon-loads of supplies, which, the thrifty woman insisted, were much cheaper in Braintree than in Philadelphia. The opulent $25,000 salary (twenty times more in today's money) barely covered their expenses for the appropriate wining and dining of officialdom. Her letters and diaries are a litany of complaints about how expensive everything was.

The older Abigail became, the more conservative she became. The ardent revolutionary was now the establishment, and she had the examples of European civility fresh in her mind. She ordered a coat of arms painted on her carriage, but John made her remove it, believing it was too excessive. She was not afraid to disagree with John either.

During a troubled and unpopular term, when foreign policy seesawed either toward France or Britain, President Adams determined to take and hold a neutral position, which alienated him from every side. (Avoiding war would subsequently be considered one of his finest gifts to the country.) Abigail did not agree. She loathed the rabble-rousing French and much preferred the stolid English. She was also in favor of the Alien and Sedition Act, which was designed to prohibit and punish adverse comments about the administration. John did not like the act, but he was persuaded to hold his nose and sign it. (That canceled out his "neutral" gift to the country.)

In their old age, cantankerous John mellowed and became downright lovable while Abigail seems to have soured. But never, never did they falter in their mutual devotion and esteem.

Postscript: ABIGAIL ADAMS WAS THE FIRST FIRST LADY TO OCCUPY THE WHITE HOUSE, ALBEIT FOR ONLY A FEW WEEKS. AMIDST THE MUD, THE WORKMEN, THE DRAFTY ROOMS THAT NEEDED ALL NINE FIREPLACES TO BE LIT CONSTANTLY, AND THE EAST ROOM FILLED WITH HER HANGING LAUNDRY, SHE MANAGED TO INJECT HER NEWFOUND DIPLOMACY AND WRY HUMOR, WRITING TO HER DAUGHTER (AFTER THE ABOVE LITANY OF COMPLAINTS), "BUT IF ANYBODY ASKS YOU, TELL THEM I SAID IT WAS LOVELY."

DOLLEY MADISON
1768–1849

FIRST LADY: 1809–17

The Magnificent

On the evening of March 4, 1809, there was a great ball in Washington City with over four hundred people in attendance. It was the grandest affair ever given in the country. James Madison had just taken the oath of office as president, and Mrs. Madison was hosting the very first inaugural ball, although she had no idea she would be starting an honored tradition. The French Minister sat on one side of the hostess, and the English Minister on the other. Normally they would not have even been in the same room. Their countries were at war. Only Dolley Madison could have inspired that maneuver.

Quaker-bred Dolley Payne Todd Madison had had years of experience as diplomatic hostess par excellence. Widowed at twenty-five, she helped run her mother's boardinghouse in Philadelphia, then the nation's capital. In residence were several congressmen, one senator, and the secretary of state. Dolley, who presided at the head of the dinner table, imposed two rules: no controversial subjects (bad for the digestion), and everyone, even the most reticent, must be included in conversation (good for politics). No one objected to the rules, and the Payne boardinghouse became a popular social center. Everyone, particularly the Virginia congressman known as Great Little Madison, wanted to meet its lovely hostess.

Their courtship was brief, and their marriage changed Dolley's life. The strict Quaker elders expelled her for marrying out of the faith, but Dolley, who was known to remark that she did not believe she had the soul of a Quaker, did not seem to mind. Now she became the "new" Dolley and could participate in the worldly things she so loved: color, music, fun, laughter, jewelry, and dessert. Madison came from a well-to-do Virginia planter family and was delighted to indulge her. Their marriage would be a particularly happy one, starting with his gift of a generations-old necklace (the first she had ever owned) and money for a trousseau of gowns in anything other than Quaker gray.

Dolley had a true talent for friendship. She sincerely liked people and enjoyed their company, and they liked her in return. She never pried or interfered, once claiming that her happiest blessing was a lack of curiosity about other peoples' business. She never gossiped. She never flirted. And despite her pleasing good looks and an engaging personality, she managed to be on excellent and even intimate terms with both men and women. Every guest invariably received the full measure of her attention. Even her in-laws adored her.

When Thomas Jefferson became president, he appointed James Madison as secretary of state. The tentative pretensions of a republican court under Washington and Adams dissolved into practically nothing under the widowed Jefferson's eight years of the gentleman's "small table." It was the home of the secretary of state that became the hub of social Washington. Dolley opened their house to guests nearly every night, and once Madison became president, that hub would henceforth and forevermore be in the White House.

As First Lady, forty-year-old Dolley was ready to initiate the Madison "large table." It may not have been Madison's personal choice, since he was a reticent man, but he adored his charming wife and was happy to oblige. He was also immensely proud and cognizant of her social skills, attributes he noticeably lacked. The White House itself was still a rude dwelling. Jefferson's domestic proclivities had been centered solely on his beloved Monticello, and the Madisons inherited a drab and drafty mansion, not far removed from Abigail Adams's days as a laundress. Having determined that the seat of government should be properly cushioned, Dolley invited several congressmen for tea and a tour of the place. That they all were members of the appropriations committee attested to her shrewdness. The First Lady gently suggested where improvements might be made, and lo and behold, funds were found for paint, draperies, carpeting, and furnishings more suitable for the home of the president.

Dolley's Legacy

Whether she intended it or not, and whether she even knew it or not, Dolley had **LEADERSHIP**. Whatever she did or didn't do was copied and imitated. Even her perceived foibles, like snuff or rouge, would be copied and imitated. Those charismatic attributes of her personality that drew people like a magnet would forever place the center of social Washington firmly in the White House. Other First Ladies might abdicate that social leadership to others, but it would hereafter be the woman of the White House who had first dibs, thanks to Mrs. Madison.

Once decorated, she opened the White House to the public. Her Wednesday evenings were religiously attended by brows high and low. It was her particular genius to mix all levels: congressmen, diplomats, military officers, clergy, merchants, the rank and file, and any decently attired citizen who was passing through town and had left his card. Women were always included. Her style stood the president in good stead, since she had a gift for remembering names and faces. A genial and delightful conversationalist in small gatherings, the shy Madison was content to let his outgoing wife take center stage.

Dolley greeted the guests herself. No platforms and no seats. She made sure everyone was introduced to someone else, and since she knew just about everyone, the introductions were always between people with commonalities. She was alert to wallflowers and carried a book with her as a conversation starter if things lagged. If she passed along important information, it was people information: nothing salacious, nasty, discriminatory, gossipy, or even politically controversial. And she never betrayed a confidence. That was the essence of Dolley's philosophy. Politics by people. She was also exceptionally aware of politics by nation. Dolley and several of her lady friends were regular observers in the congressional gallery. But she never interfered.

In an age before women's magazines, Dolley Madison was the style setter of a generation. Since she favored turban hats with ostrich feathers and yellow was her color of choice, every milliner in the country created yellow turbans. She also used rouge and took snuff, habits that ordinarily would shock polite society. But if Dolley did it, it couldn't be that terrible.

Most famous for rescuing the Gilbert Stuart full-length portrait of George Washington when the British burned the White House during the War of 1812, Dolley did something even more important only a short time later. The executive mansion had been badly burned, water damaged, and uninhabitable, but the Madisons insisted that the government would continue *in Washington*. They borrowed a nearby house suitable for their needs. The very first day they moved in, Dolley was back in business, hosting one of her receptions. The message was unmistakable: if Mrs. Madison was giving a party, then all must be well with the country. But James and Dolley Madison would never again live in the White House.

In their retirement, the Madisons' Virginia estate became a popular stopping-off place for friends, family, well-wishers, public officials of all kinds, foreign emissaries, and even strangers. With their customary hospitality, all were made welcome. But the cost of running a large plantation and the infirmities of old age took its toll. Shortly after Madison's death at eighty-five, Dolley discovered she could no longer support the place. She was nearly seventy herself and lonely. She moved back to Washington, and it is said that the day she moved into a small rented house near the executive mansion, there were more than a hundred calling cards waiting for her. Seriously impoverished, she could only afford to open her house once a month, and the refreshments were limited. But everybody came. Dolley was back where she belonged.

Postscript: WHEN DOLLEY DIED AT EIGHTY IN 1849, SHE WAS THE COUNTRY'S LAST LINK TO THE FOUNDING FATHERS. SHE HAD KNOWN THEM ALL, AND SHE HAD KNOWN THEM WELL. AND EVERYBODY LOVED DOLLEY.

LOUISA ADAMS
1775–1852

FIRST LADY: 1825–29

~~*◉◉*~~

The Shadow Lady

On paper, Louisa Catherine Johnson Adams was superbly qualified to fill not only the White House but the shoes of the illustrious Mrs. Madison. On paper, she seemed also well qualified to be the consort of the sophisticated John Quincy Adams. She was born in England to a wealthy American merchant and his British wife, educated in Paris, spoke fluent French, knew Latin and Greek, was trained in the classics, played the harp and the harpsichord, and wrote fair poetry. And she was pretty and charming to boot.

When she married John Quincy Adams in 1797, he was

the eminent son of the American vice president and on his way to becoming a well-regarded diplomat in his own right, as minister plenipotentiary to the Netherlands. Theirs had been a two-year courtship mostly by correspondence, and Louisa was given ample evidence of the cold and acerbic nature of the man she agreed to marry. He criticized and cautioned her about nearly everything, and showed little ardor. Reservations or not, the marriage took place. On their wedding day, Louisa's father confided to the bridegroom that he was bankrupt. There would be no dowry.

Nevertheless, the couple went to Prussia, a new assignment for the twenty-nine-year-old diplomat and his twenty-two-year-old bride. She was an instant hit with her cosmopolitan grace, good looks, and winsome demeanor. Louisa would be a hit wherever she went—except with her frosty husband. He doubtlessly loved her in his own way, but from the start she was relegated to the outskirts of his life, either as an ornament or as a mother. The ornament part was obvious. The mother part was not so easy. She would have fifteen pregnancies, resulting in numerous miscarriages, stillborns, and only three children who would live to maturity. It took a huge toll on her health.

After their return to America, an angst-filled appointment to the Senate, and a much-loathed stint practicing law, JQA (as he liked to refer to himself) received the plum appointment of minister plenipotentiary to Russia. (The term ambassador would not be used for nearly another century.) Louisa was torn. In some respects she wanted to return to the courtly diplomatic circles, but she agonized over leaving her two older boys, both under ten, with relatives. The Adamses would take only two-year-old Charles, and nothing would be what Louisa had expected.

Louisa's Legacy

Louisa Catherine Adams did not have the happiest of marriages, but her upbringing prepared her to conduct herself through all her trials and tribulations with unflagging **DIGNITY**. No matter what ills or unhappiness were to be her lot, she behaved appropriately, with a grace that not even the acidic John Quincy Adams could fail to recognize. There is no finer quality expected from a First Lady than dignity at all times and under all circumstances. There is also no finer example than that of Louisa Adams.

Court life in St. Petersburg was backwards and dull; she bore and buried her last child. Letters from home were scarce, the cruel and sunless Russian winters played havoc with her increasingly frail health, and the paltry and sporadically received salary of the American minister was an embarrassment compared to their European counterparts with deep pockets. Worst of all, JQA was no more attentive in St. Petersburg than he was anywhere else.

When word came that the War of 1812 had ended, JQA

was senior diplomat on the Continent and as such was dispatched to lead the peace treaty negotiations in Ghent. He left immediately, instructing his wife to sell any unneeded possessions, pack what was left, and meet him in Paris. It was a daunting challenge for the forty-year-old woman, but she managed to do it in six grueling weeks, traveling more than eighteen hundred miles through mud-mired roads scarred by years of Napoleonic wars and accompanied by dissolute, unreliable, and often dishonest servants and drivers. It was capped off by the drama of Bonaparte's escape from Elba and his march to Paris with an increasing army of motley but enthusiastic recruits. It was arguably the most important few weeks in Louisa's life. She was, for once, completely in charge of her own adventure. When she related her tale to JQA, he barely batted an eye.

John Quincy Adams was recalled home in 1817 to serve for eight years as secretary of state under James Monroe, whose wife, Elizabeth, was a haughty woman disliked and avoided by Washington society. Seemingly content with her own pretensions, First Lady Monroe pleaded the customary ill health and mostly kept to herself. Sociopolitical leadership once again fell to the secretary of state. With his eyes firmly fixed on the presidency in 1824, JQA was shrewdly aware of the importance of parlor diplomacy. He was also cognizant of his own social shortcomings and trotted Louisa out like a champion thoroughbred. She was his best asset, and he directed her to see and be seen throughout official Washington. Her eyes and ears, well tuned by years of high-level societal experience, were keen to the nuances and innuendos of casual conversation. Each day, after her calls and card leavings, Adams demanded a meticulous account of who was where and who said what. Their own house was regularly filled with the movers and shakers of officialdom. His years as secretary of state culminated in a lavish party for more than five hundred guests. One newspaper account quipped, "Belles and matrons, maids and madams, all are gone to Mrs. Adams." John Quincy Adams won the presidency, but he could not have done it without his gracious wife.

Despite Louisa's grace and charm and JQA's intellect and vision, their White House years were arguably their worst together and separately. Two venomous political campaigns left Adams with few followers and fewer friends. None of his programs, however meritorious, found sponsors. At fifty, Louisa's poor health, exacerbated by depression, female troubles, and anxiety over her older sons' dissipations, made her reclusive. Instead of the glittering social scene chez the former secretary of state, their White House parties were dull, and it is said that JQA was known to doze off at dessert. By the time they left Washington, they were barely on speaking terms. The death of their oldest son, JQA's thwarted ambitions, and the thought of returning to a detested New England law practice was a bitter pill for both.

The good people of Boston, however, had other plans for the former president. They elected him to Congress, where he would spend eighteen years and make his most important contributions. These would also be Louisa's happiest years.

They both loved Washington, where she at least had many friends. As age began to claim his eyesight (probably cataracts), JQA recruited his wife to help sort through the hundreds of letters he was receiving as the lone and wily champion of the right to petition—a forerunner of the violent antislavery feelings that would soon engulf the country. Louisa also became involved in her own correspondence with noted antislavery proponents, amazed that they actually sought *her* opinion. JQA finally achieved the admiration he lusted for all his life. Louisa finally gained *his* respect.

Postscript: LATE IN LOUISA'S LIFE, HER SON CHARLES FRANCIS RECRUITED HER ASSISTANCE IN EDITING THE LETTERS OF HIS GRANDMOTHER ABIGAIL. LOUISA AND HER MOTHER-IN-LAW HAD NEVER ENJOYED MORE THAN A LUKEWARM RELATIONSHIP. BUT THROUGH ABIGAIL'S LETTERS, LOUISA LEARNED TO VIEW THE FORMIDABLE WOMAN WITH NEW REGARD, COMMENTING, "I WISH I HAD KNOWN HER BETTER."

RACHEL JACKSON
1767–1828

Her Sacred Name

In March 1829, Andrew Jackson came to his inauguration wearing a mourning band. His voice was so low he could barely be heard. His beloved wife of more than thirty-five years had died only weeks before. They said it was her heart, which had been failing for a long time. Jackson, however, was convinced beyond doubt that she was murdered by the poisoned arrow of slander, and he would go to his grave two decades later believing nothing less.

Fourteen-year-old Rachel Donelson was a hardy girl when her large family moved from Virginia by flatboat and wagon to what is now Nashville, Tennessee. Her formal education was only rudimentary, but her domestic and survival skills compensated. At seventeen, the lively young woman with flashing black eyes married Lewis Robards, a Kentucky planter of considerable means. The marriage was doomed from the outset, since Robards had a violent temper set off by jealous rages. The couple separated on and off.

It was during one such separation that Rachel met Andrew Jackson, a young attorney new to Tennessee who was boarding with Rachel's widowed mother. Jackson was kind and sympathetic to the distraught young woman, but all agreed that their conduct was proper and above reproach.

Robards eventually had a change of heart and came to reclaim his wife. Seeing Jackson on the premises, his fury was obvious to everyone. Nevertheless, Rachel, believing it her duty, returned with her lawful husband and was subsequently subjected to more and more misery. They would separate again, this time for good.

To ease Rachel's troubles and protect her from possible retaliation from her abusive husband, Rachel was sent to visit friends in Natchez. Jackson volunteered to be among those in her escort party down the Mississippi River, ostensibly to protect them from Indians. It was on this trip that the young couple fell deeply in love. Jackson returned to Nashville and some months later read a newspaper account that Robards had obtained a divorce. Rachel was now free. Jackson hurried back to Natchez and married the former Mrs. Robards. They were both twenty-four and had known each other for three years. The large Donelson clan (there were ten siblings) adored Mr. Jackson and was delighted their sister was finally happy. And for Andrew Jackson, with not a soul of his own family, the Donelsons filled the void. He was as devoted to them as if they were his own blood. Things went well, and the Jacksons prospered.

Rachel's Legacy

Whether she intended it or not (and probably not), the shadow of Rachel Jackson even in death exerted a consuming **INFLUENCE** over her dynamic husband. The reclusive, self-effacing, gentle Rachel influenced no one else, but that one person was enough. Andrew Jackson believed to his dying day that the poisoned arrow of slander had killed his beloved wife, and he would openly champion the cause of another maligned woman, Peggy Eaton, in her memory. Cabinet members came and went, and the business of government would stall for two years under the somewhat misplaced influence of Jackson's deceased wife.

Three years later they were horrified to learn that the original news of Rachel's divorce was erroneous, and it was only then that a legal divorce had been granted on the grounds that "Rachel Robards doth live with another man." The Jacksons immediately remarried, but it was a crushing blow with deep, lifelong scars. Anger and shame overtook them; anger for him, shame for her.

The incident might have been all but forgotten in Nashville where they were both popular, but Jackson, with a volatile temperament of his own, was destined to become a public man, and public men are destined to make enemies. Those enemies—business, personal, and political—quickly learned that the surest way to Jackson's spleen was by speaking too freely on the character of Mrs. Jackson. The slightest innuendo, no matter how innocent, would fuel his rage. He fought several duels, barely avoided twice as many, and carried two bullets in his body as souvenirs—all from his unwavering resolve to protect her sacred name.

Rachel, on the other hand, turned inward. She became more and more reclusive, certain that her barren womb was divine retribution for her failed first marriage. Influenced by a local minister, her religious fervor secluded her even more. In an effort to ease the lonely woman's heartache, Jackson built her a beautiful mansion, aptly called the Hermitage. A private chapel was added for her daily devotions. A flower garden was planted where it could be seen from the veranda. Dozens of little Donelson nieces and nephews (seemingly and appropriately all named Andrew, Rachel, and Jackson) were encouraged to visit often and at length, which they were happy to do. Eventually the Jacksons adopted one of Rachel's nephews to raise as their own. But once Andrew had become General Jackson, he was away for weeks and months at a time, which only added to Rachel's loneliness and sorrow.

By the late eighteen-teens, Andrew Jackson was not only a public man but a war hero, and there was talk of the presidency in his future. Society demanded an appearance by the reluctant Mrs. J. She was loath to participate, but Old Hickory wanted her near, and as always, she wanted to please him. Each time she made the dreaded venture into Society with a capital "S", she was uncomfortable and a misfit. She had grown stout, dressed unfashionably, and her conversation was awkward and limited. In a phrase, she was out of place anywhere but in the confines of her own sheltered environment, surrounded by people who dearly loved their warm-hearted Aunt Rachel.

During Jackson's presidential campaigns, the dredged-up divorce scandal resurfaced, compounded by snide comments that Mrs. Jackson was unfit to live in the White House. It was too much for the sixty-year-old woman's failing heart. She collapsed in tears. Jackson never left her side, claiming that she had nursed him tenderly through his many illnesses and injuries over the years, and it was now his turn to tend to her. When she rallied slightly, she begged him to go rest in the next room. Then she died, sparing him the pain of witnessing her last breath.

Rachel Jackson was buried in her beloved flower garden, wearing the white gown she had intended for Jackson's inauguration. Her husband said that he forgave his enemies, but those who slandered his beloved Rachel would have to look to God alone for forgiveness.

Postscript: ANDREW JACKSON WORE RACHEL'S MINIATURE ON A CHAIN AROUND HIS NECK FOR THE REST OF HIS LIFE. HER PORTRAIT AND BIBLE WERE ON A TABLE NEXT TO HIS BED, SO IT WOULD BE THE LAST THING HE WOULD SEE AT NIGHT AND THE FIRST THING UPON AWAKENING. HE PLANTED A MAGNOLIA TREE ON THE WHITE HOUSE LAWN IN HER MEMORY. IT STILL STANDS THERE TODAY.

JULIA TYLER
1820–89

FIRST LADY: 1844–45

~~~

The Rose of Long Island

When John Tyler became president in 1841, the White House had been without a First Lady for twelve years. Widower Andrew Jackson had invited nieces to do his honors. The daughter-in-law of widower Martin Van Buren did his honors. Anna Harrison, pushing seventy, planned to wait for the spring thaw before she plodded east from Indiana, but her plans were scrapped when her equally aged husband died only a month into his presidency.

Vice president-turned-president Tyler came to the White House with seven children between eleven and twenty-five and a bedridden wife, who would succumb some months later. Into the void whirled Julia Gardiner, the Rose of Long Island, a soubriquet given her by a New York merchant when he used her likeness on an advertising handbill.

Julia was pretty, cultured, spoiled, trained to charm—and very, *very* rich. She could and did have her pick of suitors among Washington's bigwigs. It would be the sitting president himself who picked her, even though he was thirty years her senior. As was fashionable, Julia played hard to get, turning him down just as she had deterred other elderly suitors. But Tyler, at fifty-four, was still attractive, athletic, financially comfortable, and an ardent Southern courtier, romantic to the core. He kept pursuing. She kept fluttering her fan and demurring. But the seeds had been planted. Being president, even the unpopular one that he was, ranked high on the plus side.

The turning point came via a terrible accident. The gunboat *Princeton* was demonstrating its new weaponry on a presidential party cruise down the Potomac when the gun misfired and killed several people, including Julia's father. The president's solicitous attentions and condolences finally won over the daddy's girl who had just lost her daddy, and the two eloped a few months later. Naturally, tongues wagged throughout Washington over the May-December marriage, calling Tyler either an old fool or "Lucky John." It seems he was Lucky John. It would prove to be a happy and productive union. Seven more little Tylers would make appearances.

With the new, beautiful, and very wealthy Mrs. Tyler

gracing the White House, things began to change. Gardiner money poured in, renovating and refurbishing a place that had been neglected since the Monroe administration a quarter of a century earlier. "I have commenced my auspicious reign and am in quiet possession of the Presidential Mansion," she wrote. Despite observing the decorum of her bereavement, genteel receptions, dinners, and parties of all sorts, which had been characteristic of Tyler's Southern hospitality, now became cosmopolitan and elegant. She introduced waltzes and polkas, hitherto considered shocking—at least in Washington. Copying the trends of Europe, which Julia had experienced firsthand (when her family whisked her away after the scandalous Rose of Long Island business), she invited friends and relatives to serve as her maids of honor at receptions. They all dressed in color-coordinated gowns and posed dramatically as the living centerpiece for the event. Very la-di-dah.

Julia's own trousseau was expensive, extensive, and glamorous. Her trademark jeweled tiara, which she wore across her forehead, became the rage. She was as much a style setter as the aging and legendary Dolley Madison, whom Julia was thrilled to host on numerous occasions.

The new Mrs. T. was drawn to the spotlight like a moth to flame. She appeared on the streets of Washington walking an Italian greyhound on a leash. If she drove, it was in an elegant coach pulled by six white horses, certain to attract attention. She sat in the visitors gallery to attend congressional debates, making an entrance with her usual flair. She was also known to solicit political appointments. President T. occasionally obliged. He was as delighted with his trophy wife as she was with her trophy husband. He was happy to indulge her at every opportunity.

Julia T.'s Legacy

Julia Tyler was young and pretty and rich. She brought a **PANACHE** to the White House that would not be seen again until Jacqueline Kennedy became First Lady more than a century later. Whether it was wearing a diamond tiara across her forehead, walking greyhounds down Pennsylvania Avenue, or creating fatuous French tableaux, if it was stylish, Julia T. would embrace it to the hilt. Glitz and glamour have long been associated with the seat of power, but few First Ladies had the ability to dazzle. Julia T. could dazzle.

The country might have enjoyed this revival of flamboyance, but Julia's time as First Lady only lasted nine months. Tyler's independent politics left him a man without a party, despite some grand-scale partying. Their last big shindig was said to have cost Tyler more than 10 percent of his yearly salary. But it did not make him any more popular. Not only was he *not* reelected, he wasn't even renominated.

Disappointed but far from crushed, ex-President and Mrs.

Tyler moved to his beautiful plantation in tidewater Virginia, where the Rose of Long Island transformed herself into an adopted daughter of Dixie. Despite the neighbors looking askance at the Yankee transplant at first, she fit in with her usual confident style, happy to host her turn at the barbecues, suppers, and picnics. Fifteen years of plenty followed. Plenty of money, plenty of travel, plenty of happiness, and plenty of children. Even plenty of hope that the ex-president might once again be called upon to lead the country. Then came the Civil War, and seventy-one-year-old Tyler was elected to the Confederate Congress, but he promptly died before taking his seat.

Fifteen years of ruin followed. Two of her sons, still in their teens, served in the Rebel army. With her younger children still babies, she was persuaded to "flee North" to her family when George B. McClellan's army threatened the Virginia Peninsula not far from her beloved Sherwood Forest plantation. She was by then not only a proud rebel but a loud one, and she made herself totally obnoxious in New York by her openly Confederate sympathies and overt activities. The war also proved hazardous to her Virginia home, which was left a sorry mess. She lost most of her money. Relatives died or were estranged. Legal chaos was still to be untangled. Poor Julia. Literally. She spent years lobbying Congress for reparations and a pension as a presidential widow (not withstanding her avowed affection for the Confederacy). Congress took its own sweet time about it. As the infirmities of age (nearly seventy) and misfortune took its toll, she left her plantation in the hands of her children and moved a short distance away to Richmond. In a stroke of irony, she died in the same hotel her husband had died in nearly thirty years earlier.

Postscript: THE COUNTRY SEEMED TO REMEMBER HER FLAMBOYANCE AND FORGET HER CONFEDERATE SYMPATHIES IN HER LATER YEARS. SHE ACTUALLY WAS INVITED TO A FEW SHINDIGS AT THE WHITE HOUSE.

SARAH POLK
1803–91

FIRST LADY: 1845–49

Sarah, Straight and Strong

Modern historians, especially female ones, love to claim Sarah Polk as an unheralded First Lady whose abilities, intelligence, and four years of wearing two hats go largely unnoticed. They are, of course, absolutely right to do so.

Sarah Childress was brought up akin to Abigail Adams in a prosperous household where education—including for women—was encouraged. She learned early on all the domestic skills needed for household management, but just as early on, she decided that housekeeping was not her thing. She attended one of the best female academies in the South, learning the classics and developing a sincere interest in politics. In early nineteenth-century Tennessee, where she was born and raised, rough-and-tumble politics was as popular as a sporting event.

When twenty-something James Knox Polk was considering matrimony, his mentor, none other than Old Hickory himself, counseled him to "look no further than Miss Sarah Childress." It was sound advice. Not only did the couple marry, but they were particularly well suited and enjoyed a happy union for a quarter of a century.

There would be no Polk offspring, and like many childless couples, they drew closer together. Lack of children (something Sarah never seemed to miss like Aunt Rachel) also kept her untroubled by the various birthing-related ailments that plagued many of her contemporaries. With good health and no family needs at home, Sarah was free to travel frequently with her husband who enjoyed her companionship, especially since he was another one of our presidents who was notably lackluster in the social department.

Social or not, Polk served in Congress (and was even Speaker of the House for a while) throughout Jackson's presidency, and Sarah and he took up boardinghouse residence, as was customary. She was one of the few women who accompanied their congressional husbands, but she made friends readily, even with the grande dames, those Washington residents who remained permanently while officialdom came and went. Polk's colleagues seemed to like Sarah well enough too—usually better than they liked him. He was a small, unimposing

SARAH POLK | 41

man, a bit like Madison in appearance. He was a hard worker, no question, but he was primarily a loner.

Polk's political career was unremarkable and had its ups and downs: after his time in Congress, a single term as Tennessee governor, and then two reelection losses. By 1844 he was all but forgotten. In a last ditch effort to keep from practicing law (which he disliked almost as much as John Quincy Adams did), he "encouraged" others to float his name as candidate for vice president, an honorable position, but requiring no heavy lifting. Politics being politics, he became president instead, the country's first successful dark horse candidate. That this unknown managed to win against political icon Henry Clay puzzled many, and it is generally believed that Clay *lost,* rather than that Polk *won.* Nevertheless, James Knox Polk became the eleventh president and pledged to pursue a monumental agenda, all to be completed in a single term.

Sarah was a handsome woman of forty-two with no inclination for housekeeping. Now she was mistress of a great house and promptly hired someone to manage the day-to-day chores. A thrifty soul, she had no plans to redecorate the mansion. "What's good enough for the Tylers is good enough for us," she supposedly said, although she did splurge and had gaslights installed to replace the old-fashioned candles, which she kept anyway—just in case.

Herein lies part of the reason that Sarah, for all her political acumen and intelligence, fails to make the First Lady A-list: she was as humorless as her husband, and nondomestic or not, she bowed to the conventional mores of the 1840s.

Not a feisty bone in her body. She behaved exactly as society expected: quietly charming and gracious without calling undue attention to herself. Her opinions were reserved for her husband's ears alone. Deeply rooted in her Presbyterian faith, she nixed dancing, billiards, wine, music, and card playing in the White House. She was also a devout Sabbatarian. No guests on Sundays, unless they wished to accompany the Polks to church.

Above all, the Polks were frugal to the point of being stingy. James Polk hoped to bank a large portion of his annual $25,000 salary, which was considered sumptuous in a day when $1,200 a year could raise a family comfortably. Since all expenses for entertaining, travel, and secretarial assistance came from the presidential purse, there was plenty of fat to be cut.

Neither of them approved of or took spirits, for instance, ergo they felt no need to provide it for others. As it would be thirty years later, the White House was bone dry. They also believed that their public receptions and meet-and-greet events were a part of the job, performed as an agenda item rather than a social courtesy. They did not believe that providing refreshments was on that agenda. Not only would there be no spirits, but there would be no coffee, tea, or fruit punch. No food, no cakes, no cookies. The traditionally generous hospitality of other Southern first families was lost on the Southern-ish Polks. In summer, however, they made an exception. If any visitor was foolish enough—like themselves—to stay in the disease-ridden sweltering climate of Washington, the Polks were kind enough to offer them ice water. People said nice things about Sarah, but they also said her parties were deadly dull.

Sarah's Legacy

Sarah Polk was a serious woman, and like her equally serious husband, she brought a sense of **DILIGENCE** to the role of First Lady. They both believed that their high office demanded their utmost attention, time, and labor. Both of them worked tirelessly, taking little if any recreation, and rendering their best efforts. Other First Ladies have taken their position seriously, and in more modern days, they have expanded the role exponentially, but Sarah was the first to understand the active work of being First Lady rather than merely its social importance. Even in her retirement, Sarah organized and sorted her husband's papers, ensuring that they would be preserved for posterity.

With plenty of time on her hands and another opportunity to economize, Sarah donned a second hat: private secretary to her husband. It would save them nearly $2,000 a year. (Prior to that, several presidents had engaged young male relatives to keep the records straight and keep the money in the family.)

Educated, literate, smart, and politically astute, Sarah could copy Polk's papers in a clear hand, maintain the files and appointment book, and perhaps, most important, read the incoming mail and newspapers and summarize or underscore the salient parts. Disinclined to delegate, both Polks put in twelve- to fifteen-hour days with no time off, except for Sunday. They believed that since providence had placed them in such a high position, it was incumbent upon them to place duty and hard work above all else. In four years, they only left the White House once for relaxation—and that was for a weekend trip.

Polk accomplished every item on his ambitious agenda in his lone four-year term, but it cost him dearly. Always delicate in health, he died three months after leaving office. Overwork and exhaustion were speculated. Sarah went back to Tennessee. She never left her house except to go to church.

Postscript: FOR THE REST OF HER NEARLY NINETY YEARS, MRS. POLK ALWAYS REMAINED POPULAR WITH POLITICIANS OF ALL PARTIES. DIGNITARIES VISITING NASHVILLE USUALLY STOPPED BY TO TAKE TEA WITH THE VENERABLE MRS. P., WHO BY THAT TIME OFFERED REFRESHMENTS.

THREE RECLUSIVES
AND MISS LANE

MARGARET TAYLOR (1788–1852)

Margaret Taylor (1849–50) came to the White House not only by surprise but against her will. If she is remembered at all, it is only by her prophecy: "It will shorten both our lives."

Margaret Smith was born in Maryland to a good plantation family, and at twenty-one she married Zachary Taylor, a professional soldier who was destined to rise through the ranks. As a soldier's wife along the frontier of the early nineteenth century, Peggy, as she was called, endured the hardships of military life, staying in garrison barracks, tents, lean-tos, shacks, and wherever camp was made. It was a simple, rugged life with few gracious amenities. She bore six children and buried three. When they were old enough for schooling, they were sent back east to live with relatives.

During the Mexican War, Zachary Taylor, now a general, became a national hero, and in those days of turbulent politics, the hero business bumped him up to a potentially viable Whig candidate in 1848. Taylor didn't agree and said so. He knew and cared little about politics and never cast a ballot in his life (and that would include his own election). The Whigs thought differently. They told him to keep quiet and let them handle things. He did and they did, and he was elected. Peggy issued her prophesy.

She was livid. At sixty, she had grown stout with the usual aches and pains of age and harsh living. It had only been a few years since the Taylors had finally been able to purchase their first home—a modest plantation in Louisiana where she wished to live out the rest of her days in peace and quiet.

The White House was no place for an aging woman whose social acumen and graces had long been eroded by hard frontier life. Unequipped and unwilling to be the leader of society, and perhaps fearful of criticism and ridicule, she asked one of her daughters to do the honors and retired upstairs to preside only at the family table.

Postscript: PEGGY'S PREDICTION WAS ACCURATE. ZACHARY TAYLOR DIED OF NATURAL CAUSES IN 1850, AND SHE DIED A YEAR AND A HALF LATER. NEITHER COMPLETED THE FOUR-YEAR PRESIDENTIAL TERM.

ABIGAIL FILLMORE (1798–1853)

It is a pity that Abigail Fillmore (1850–53) chose to withdraw from most of the duties of First Ladyhood. She was an intelligent, bookish woman who was the first First Lady to have been employed outside the home. Abigail Powers had become a schoolteacher at sixteen in Upstate New York, obliged to help support her family. Millard Fillmore was a farm boy near her own age who became her student.

Their engagement lasted seven years, as Abigail continued teaching while Fillmore completed his education and began to rise as a lawyer and a mediocre Whig congressman. Of course, after they married and had children, Abigail was expected to stay home, so she did. Still, she remained intellectually active and became a founding member of their local library, not far from Buffalo. She also played the harp and the piano and managed to teach herself French.

The few documented items specifically connected to Abigail Fillmore are library wish lists of books that her husband would purchase as he passed through New York City and Philadelphia on his trips to and from Congress. She chose to remain at home during Fillmore's congressional career, and she only joined him in Washington when he became vice president in 1849. She quickly learned to dislike Washington's hypercritical, gossipy society. It also bored her. Then Zachary Taylor died.

Once again, the presidency was a total and unwelcome surprise for a new First Lady. A few years earlier she had fallen and broken her ankle, which was poorly set and caused her chronic discomfort. Thus armed with a ready excuse for avoiding receiving lines and meeting and greeting a great many people she did not like, she participated as seldom as possible. Her twenty-year-old daughter usually pinch-hit.

Abigail Fillmore did leave one fine legacy. Once moved into the White House, she was dismayed to learn there wasn't a book in the entire place—not even a Bible. She urged her husband to request funds for books for the president's use, and Congress accommodated to the tune of $250, a substantial sum in 1850. Abigail the teacher-librarian was delighted to compile lists of all the books she thought appropriate, and it is said that when the packages arrived, she carefully opened each box and lovingly put the books on the shelves.

It would have been nice to know Abigail Fillmore a little better.

Postscript: ANXIOUS TO RETURN HOME AFTER MILLARD'S PRESIDENCY, THE FILLMORES PLANNED TO STAY FOR THE PIERCE INAUGURATION AND THEN HEAD BACK TO BUFFALO. UNFORTUNATELY, ABIGAIL CAUGHT A COLD AT THE CEREMONIES. IT TURNED INTO PNEUMONIA, AND SHE DIED IN A WASHINGTON HOTEL TWO WEEKS LATER.

JANE PIERCE (1806–63)

A New England minister-educator's daughter, Jane Appleton (1853–57) was consumptive and depressive by nature and "morbidly religious" by inclination. In other words, she embraced the gloomy side of everything, believing in a punishing deity, and that true happiness could only be found in the afterlife. This was the polar opposite of her outgoing, gregarious husband, congressman and later senator Franklin Pierce. He tried hard to please her, but as one biographer claims, Jane found it easier to criticize than to praise. The few historians who have concentrated on Pierce are generally sympathetic to him, perhaps understanding the reasons he was known to bend an elbow from time to time.

Jane stayed in Washington briefly while Pierce served in Congress. She hated politics, spent most of the time in her room, and it is believed was instrumental in her husband's withdrawal from the national arena. He opened a mediocre law practice and concentrated his political activity solely in their small New Hampshire community and even declined a cabinet position in Polk's administration.

Jane was generally contented in her tiny cocoon. They had three sons; two died as babies. Their third son, born when Jane was in her late thirties, was her last chance at motherhood, and she devoted herself exclusively to little Bennie, smothering him with attention, and replicating in him her own fears and religious convictions. Franklin Pierce's nomination as president in 1852 was another surprise—to the entire country if not to Pierce himself. Having been out of the public eye for a decade, he was another dark horse, electable *because* he was unknown. He was also considered one of the few Northern candidates acceptable to the South. When Jane found out, she fainted. When she came to, she was very distressed.

Then tragedy struck. Shortly before the inauguration, there was a train accident, and eleven-year-old Bennie was instantly killed. Jane would never recover. First she got it into her head that God was punishing them for leaving home; then she decided that their son was taken so Pierce would not be distracted from his presidential duties. Either way, the episode weighed heavily on both of them for the rest of their lives.

Jane opted out of the First Lady business, retreating into her deep mourning. Her aunt by marriage came to Washington to help an also-mourning president fulfill his social obligations. So did Mrs. Jefferson Davis, the wife of Pierce's good friend and secretary of war. The one account of Jane at a social function cites her "woebegone expression" that made it impossible for anyone to enjoy themselves. Jane spent the next four years writing letters to her dead son, begging him to put in a good word for her in the afterlife.

Postscript: THINKING A CHANGE OF SCENERY WOULD HELP, PIERCE TOOK HIS WIFE TO EUROPE AFTER HIS TERM WAS OVER. IT DIDN'T. AS THEIR GOOD FRIEND NATHANIEL HAWTHORNE WOULD WRITE, "JANE WASN'T REALLY OF THIS WORLD."

HARRIET LANE (1830-1903)

Then came Miss Harriet Lane (1857–61), whose glittering social success was diametrically opposed to the failed presidency of her uncle, James Buchanan. When she was orphaned at the age of nine, Uncle Buck (or "Nunc," as she called him) took Harriet as his ward. She was devoted to him and he to her. He made sure she was clothed and educated in the best possible manner. Since bachelor Buchanan was of comfortable means, this was not hard.

During the Pierce administration, elder statesman James Buchanan was appointed minister to England, where he and his twenty-one-year-old niece proceeded to charm everyone. Miss Harriet was pretty, innocent, conventional according to the customs and traditions of the day, and could curtsey gracefully to Queen Victoria. She was disinclined to make waves.

Like Pierce, it was precisely *because* of his absence from the scene for four turbulent years that Buchanan was elected president in 1856. On the plus side, he was a Northerner from Pennsylvania with a long résumé of competent public service, and he was acceptable to Southerners. On the other hand, he was nearly seventy, considered a "Miss Nancy" in his manners, and totally unequipped for the wrenching turmoil that awaited him. Harriet Lane, however, was completely equal to her task as White House hostess, if not de facto First Lady.

She was twenty-five and by then experienced in the details and nuances of gracious entertaining on a high level. Her clothes were fashionable, her manners impeccable. Thrust into a society where her companions were usually old enough to be her mother, she glided through Washington with aplomb, charming everyone. She provided a sparkling social setting unseen since the days of Dolley Madison a half century earlier.

The young Prince of Wales (later Edward VII) danced with her at the White House ball she arranged in his honor, and the song "Listen to the Mockingbird" was dedicated to her. She accepted no gifts other than flowers or candy, offended no one, and was well thought of by everyone, even the harshest critics of the Buchanan administration and the carping dowagers of Washington society. Buchanan may have been a total flop, but Harriet was a whopping success!

Postscript: COMPLETELY DEVOTED TO NUNC DURING HIS PRESIDENCY, HARRIET DID NOT MARRY UNTIL SHE WAS THIRTY-FIVE, SEVERAL YEARS AFTER SHE LEFT THE WHITE HOUSE.

MARY LINCOLN
1818–82

FIRST LADY: 1861–65

The Born Diva

In an age when wives, not just presidential wives, were given passing if not glowing grades in deportment, Mary Todd Lincoln was the exception: she was overtly and strongly disliked by most of her contemporaries and most definitely by those who knew her best.

Born to whatever aristocratic purple early Kentucky could claim, Mary Todd was third-generation born in Lexington. Her large, pedigreed, well-heeled, and well-connected family provided her with an excellent finishing school education, complete with French, coquetry, and ambition. By the time of her marriage to Abraham Lincoln in 1842, three sisters, a few cousins, and several kin of kin were making similar purple claims in Springfield, Illinois.

In a figurative sense, Mary brought the tablecloth to a very humble Lincoln table. If he were to rise in his profession, he would need the proper setting. His marriage to Mary polished his manners. She saw to it that his coat and hat were brushed, his shoes shined, and his shirts clean. She taught him to dance a little, to bow gracefully, and to balance a teacup on his lanky knees. She bore him four sons. One died as a baby. Their Springfield house was small in comparison to others, but it was decorated according to the tastes of the day. Mary did her own sewing and cooking, and she was happy to entertain Lincoln's political friends. She had always liked politics, and she was intuitive and sharp in her observations. Whatever her failings, they were private within the family.

Thus, when she became First Lady in early 1861, she was, at least in her own mind, well prepared to take up the duties of society leadership that had recently been ably filled by Harriet Lane. What Mary didn't know, however, was that she already had three strikes against her, and whatever failings she may have brought along would now be public.

The Civil War, of course, polarized the country. Lincoln himself was unpopular; seven Southern states had already seceded, and four more were on the way. Actual warfare was within earshot. Washington had always been a Southern town in its manners and influences. To the Northerners, Mary was definitely a Southerner. After all, her family were slave owners. Three brothers, a brother-in-law, a few cousins, and more kin of kin fought and some would die for the Confederacy. Many Northerners were convinced that Mary was a Rebel spy. She wasn't.

Mary's Legacy

Mary Lincoln did not have a successful First Ladyhood. She was neither liked nor admired, and in truth she was meddlesome and an impediment in many ways. Her list of faults outweighs her list of virtues. But her legacy is one for the country rather than for the role of First Lady. Mary was truly **FRAGILE** and needed care. If Congress had given her the full four years of Lincoln's salary, as she wanted and pleaded for, it would have been money well spent. She could have paid her debts, purchased a modest house, and retired in comparative seclusion. The politicians after the Civil War wanted her to disappear on the cheap, however. The country would regret its collective behavior, since no presidential widow, with or without fragility or need, would ever be so badly treated again.

To Southerners, Kentucky-bred and Illinois-wed Mary was a Westerner: a woman of low taste. Granted, she lacked the sophistication of some of her Eastern peers, but Mary was not without breeding. Finally, it was no secret that Lincoln was a man of lowly origins. Many Washingtonians, particularly the society dames, assumed he had married a woman of his own station. Mary knew otherwise and let them know it. She did nothing to further her own popularity. Indeed, whatever she did, no matter how well meaning, only served to isolate herself from the very people who might have befriended her.

Now in her early forties, Mary had eagerly wanted to be First Lady, and she rejoiced at Lincoln's election. She had been well educated, certainly more so than her husband, and in both Lexington and Springfield, she was considered the upper crust. Social pretensions were as much a part of the Todd family as the second *d* in their name (although one *d* was good enough for God, according to Lincoln).

Mary's girlhood friendships, whatever there were, had fallen away, which is not uncommon when one marries and paths drift. Her relationships with her sisters yo-yoed throughout her life, but they were never particularly close. Much has been said and written about the volatile Mrs. L. and her angry outbursts, ill-tempered tongue, and nearly pathological spending habits, which became more apparent and certainly more public in Washington. Lincoln's secretary John Hay called her a "Hellcat." Most family members kept a safe distance. A fair-sized contingent of Todd kin came to the inaugural festivities, stayed briefly, and then went home. One cousin was prevailed upon to stay and keep Mary company, but after a few months that grew burdensome, and she secretly begged to be rescued via a concocted family emergency. In a phrase common among Victorians, Mary's husband had become "her all."

So poor Mary, with no real friends and a desperate "I'll show them" need, was left to her own devices. The president, her husband, "her all," was beset by the growing crises of a civil war and had little time to devote to her. He also had little inclination toward women things, particularly social pretensions. Society matrons avoided Mary and were conspicuously absent from her soirees. She was imperious, self-centered, and disdainful of them. The men who did frequent her receptions were, for the most part, the wrong sort: those who hoped to profit from Mary's supposed influence. They soon learned how susceptible she was to flattery, and they laid it on with a trowel, not knowing that her influence was negligible.

A year later, battered by a bitter war, snubbed by society, neglected by an overworked husband, and lonely beyond her own insights, Mary lost her second son. She completely fell apart and, abiding by Victorian customs for women, took up prolonged and intense mourning rituals. These customs also encouraged spiritualism, which Mary embraced wholeheartedly in an effort to find some comfort. Now at least, if Mary couldn't have friendship or affection, perhaps she could have pity.

Pity is a funny thing. It works very well for a time and then it palls. By the time Mary emerged from her loss some two years later, a new and more dreadful loss would traumatize her: the assassination of her husband, "her all," before her eyes. If she had fallen apart with the death of her son, this tragedy would shatter her fragile emotions completely, and she would never recover.

The pity wore thin very quickly this time. After all, few families in the country were without lost husbands and fathers and sons. Officials in Washington were thoroughly drained by the angst of four years of war and wanted to move on. They had also grown to dislike this self-absorbed woman who wailed loudly and wept incessantly in a claim for center stage. Other women wept quietly, and then dried their tears and picked up the pieces. Not Mary. Since she would not go away, she was pushed away.

Mary was literally homeless. Her Springfield house held too many memories. It was sold. Mary couldn't afford to keep a house of her own. She had monumental debts to pay to the merchants who dunned her relentlessly, and Congress was unforgivably stingy. Lincoln's estate was decent enough, but Mary only received a third; her two remaining sons were entitled to their inheritance. Finally, her own disposition was such that nobody could live with her. So she was a wanderer.

The country, whether it liked her or not, treated Mary Lincoln shamefully. It would never again treat a presidential widow so badly.

Postscript: FEW HISTORIANS HAVE EVER REMAINED NEUTRAL ABOUT MARY LINCOLN. SOME OFFER PROLONGED APOLOGIES FOR "MISUNDERSTANDING" HER; OTHERS CREDIT HER WITH TRULY BEING THE "HELL-CAT" THAT JOHN HAY CLAIMED. THE TRUTH NO DOUBT LIES IN THE MIDDLE, LIKE IT ALWAYS DOES. BUT NONE OF THE EARLY FIRST LADIES, NOT EVEN ELEANOR ROOSEVELT, HAVE INSPIRED MORE BIOGRAPHIES.

JULIA GRANT
1826–1902

FIRST LADY: 1869–77

Rock Solid to the Core

Mark Twain called it the Gilded Age, an opulent economic phoenix rising from the ashes of a shattered country. Over-the-top elegance, splendor, and whatever money could buy was considered the key to good living. The Grants, unpretentious at heart but willing to learn, would become the most popular presidential couple since George and Martha Washington. After the war-torn Lincoln administration with a disliked Mary, followed by an equally disliked Andrew Johnson and his tubercular wife, Eliza, it was not difficult to be popular.

Julia Dent was born outside of St. Louis, Missouri, to a

comfortably middle-class slaveholding family. Her education was mediocre. She went to boarding school in town, but she was never considered a scholar. Stocky and plain with a crossed-eye condition, she nevertheless possessed a pleasant and accommodating personality. Throughout her life, she would make friends wherever she went.

She married Bvt. Capt. Ulysses S. Grant, her brother's West Point classmate, when she was twenty-two, after a four-year secret engagement by correspondence. The marriage would be one of the happiest among first families. She provided her taciturn and generally undistinguished husband with the loyal, uncomplaining support and devotion that was imperative to his well-being.

Four years into their marriage, Grant resigned from the army after a bad bout of homesickness and alcohol threatened his career. Then ten years of bad-to-worse luck followed with little prospects of success. Julia was doing her own housework and cooking, raising four children, and foregoing any luxuries. But she never reproved her husband—not even by a silent look. She believed in his inherent greatness. She was probably the only one who did, and hers was a true love.

When the Civil War began, Grant was a lowly clerk at his father's tannery in Galena, Illinois. Reinstated in the Union army shortly after the surrender of Fort Sumter, his rise was an up-and-down progression of victories and inactivity, loyally accompanied by Julia and the kids, who joined him whenever and wherever possible. They traveled by wagon, stagecoach, carriage, train, and steamboat. They stayed in hotels, boardinghouses, with friends, and in Grant's camp tents. Once Vicksburg was safely in Union hands, General Grant found himself in the hero business. Following Robert E. Lee's surrender at Appomattox Court House, he was *the* hero, arguably the most famous man in the country.

Gifts for the Great General and Mrs. Grant started pouring in from a grateful nation even before the war's end, and not merely wagonloads of cigars and flowers. They received elegant carriages and thoroughbred horses, jeweled swords, gold trays, enough silver to rival the Comstock lode, and most important, an unending stream of invitations from the rich and powerful, all of whom were anxious to host and befriend the hero. Private citizen and Mrs. Grant were happy to accept all of the above, sincerely believing that it would be rude and ungracious to decline such hospitality and generosity, even from those industrialists who were being derided as robber barons. (It could also be conjectured that Grant was thrilled to finally give his wife all the things he couldn't afford to give her before.) They would be given a house in Philadelphia (because they had once considered living there), a house in Galena (which claimed Grant as its own), a house in Washington where they actually lived for a while, and even a summer cottage in Long Branch, New Jersey (deeded to Julia when Grant declined it as being excessive). The culmination of course, was the best house the country could offer: the White House.

The country was delighted with the forty-three-year-old Julia Grant. Still plain and even dowdy in comparison to just about everybody, she appreciated the cosmopolitan socialites who offered to befriend her and put her fashionable new gowns on their personal accounts. Congress gave her tantamount to a blank check for elaborate redecorating according to Gilded Age standards, and the Grant White House was thrown open for entertaining. Their receptions and dinners were elegant, happy affairs, all the more charming since President Grant always retained his innate understated modesty and Julia her essential niceness. She would learn to put on airs with the best of them, but they would always be airs of her acquired status and never of personal snobbishness. Everyone seemed to be comfortable in her company.

The pinnacle of the gifts and airs turned out to be the White House wedding of their seventeen-year-old daughter Nellie to a titled (albeit alcoholic) Englishman. It was the first White House wedding in decades, and presents poured in from all over the world, including, it is said, a handkerchief valued at more than $500 in Gilded Age pre-tax money.

After their White House tenancy, Julia and her hero spent two years touring the world. Now they would be wined, dined, and gifted by kings, queens, emperors, kaisers, tsars, and even the mikado of Japan. But gifts are not money, and when Grant's money ran out, they came home. Bowing to the advice of his supporters, Grant halfheartedly sought a third presidential term, but it fizzled. Julia, who truly wanted a return White House engagement, was disappointed.

Once more, their finest days were when bad-and-worse luck was upon them. Needing a steady income, and guilty only of naiveté and poor business judgment, Grant was seduced into a financial brokerage venture. His partner was a total scoundrel who devised a Ponzi scheme, absconded with several hundred thousand dollars, and left Grant holding the bag. The Great General, whose personal integrity was never in question, insisted that all the debts would be paid. Shortly after that fiasco, he was diagnosed with terminal cancer of the throat.

Julia G.'s Legacy

Few presidents have had a more up-and-down career than Ulysses Grant, and through it all, thick and thin, there was Julia, whose **ADAPTABILITY** was the keystone of her husband's life. In good times and in some very bad times, you could plunk her anywhere and she would make it a home. Whether it was as an army wife, an impoverished farmer's wife, an unhappy clerk's wife, a great general's wife, or First Lady, Julia was wife first. She could put down roots and thrive wherever she was. Every First Lady needs to acclimate to new surroundings and new challenges. It is even better if they can flourish wherever they land. Some do it better than others.

Julia never left his side, nor did she ever weep in his presence. To repay the brokerage debts, all the Grant houses were sold, including Julia's childhood home that they had inherited after her father died. The swords, trays, gifts from foreign dignitaries, and even his Civil War memorabilia were assigned to his creditors. Finally, in an effort to keep Julia from want and his children from obligation, Grant began writing his war memoirs. A week after the galleys were completed, he died.

Unlike Mary Lincoln, Julia Grant would be a very rich widow. Grant's book earned more than $300,000 in the first year alone. She outlived her husband by seventeen years and even wrote her *own* memoirs, the first First Lady ever to do so. The handwritten manuscript was not discovered until seventy-five years after her death, locked in a trunk in a granddaughter's attic.

Postscript: IF GALENA, ILLINOIS, CLAIMED GRANT IN LIFE, NEW YORK CITY CLAIMED HIM IN DEATH. GRANT'S WILL EXPLICITLY DIRECTED THAT HIS BELOVED JULIA BE BURIED BY HIS SIDE, WHERE SHE HAD LAIN FOR NEARLY FORTY YEARS. THEY ARE BOTH BURIED IN GRANT'S TOMB.

LUCY HAYES
1831–89

FIRST LADY: 1877–81

The Old-Fashioned New Woman

Lucy Webb was the quintessential old-fashioned girl from Ohio. Left fatherless as a baby, she was raised by a mother who was decidedly *not* old-fashioned. Mrs. Webb was a staunch admirer of feminist educator Mary Lyon and believed strongly that women should receive "higher learning." Lucy, whether she wanted to or not, did not go to a traditional finishing school for girls, but an academic female seminary that is now connected with Ohio Wesleyan. There she learned the classics, Greek and Latin, geometry, science, history, and philosophy, at a time when teaching such advanced subjects to women was controversial and even ridiculed. She was an apt student, but she had no ambitions.

At twenty, Lucy married Rutherford B. Hayes, who was ten years her senior. Also raised by a widowed mother, he had become a lawyer, thanks in large part to the generosity and mentoring of his uncle Sardis Birchard. The Hayeses' marriage would be conventional, happy, and fruitful. Five of their eight children would survive to adulthood.

Lucy's Legacy

Whether or not it was her personal decision to ban spirits in the White House, Lucy unquestionably subscribed to the practice. Always deeply religious, her well-publicized **MORAL SUASION** regarding temperance and strict Sabbath observation may have been mocked by some, but by and large she was perceived as an upstanding example of womanhood and well beloved by most. Her retirement years were spent in charitable activities. Every First Lady exerts a fair amount of moral example, whether overtly or in personal practice. Lucy's morality was sincere, just more visible.

"Rud" Hayes was past forty and their family well underway when the Civil War began, but like many others at the time, he enlisted immediately and would rise to become a brevet major general. His was not merely a political or administrative command; Hayes served in the field and was wounded four times, once seriously. With Hayes's wealthy and benevolent Uncle Sardis acting as surrogate grandfather, Lucy was free to join her husband in camp as often as possible, especially when he had been wounded. Her personal care freed other nurses to tend to other casualties. The soldiers and fellow officers alike grew to love the gentle lady who was happy to mother them and mend their uniforms. Rutherford and Lucy Hayes would always be beloved among the soldiers of the 23rd Ohio Infantry and would remain active in veteran affairs until they died.

Multi-wounded generals, especially lawyers and Republicans, were prime candidates for public office at the end of the Civil War, and Ohio Republicans duly elected Hayes to Congress and later made him governor of Ohio.

By the time Hayes was nominated for the presidency in 1876, Lucy was forty-six and past childbearing. Always a devout Methodist, she was proud that she had remained the old-fashioned girl of her youth. Her hairstyle never changed: parted in the center and pulled back into a bun. Her dresses remained modest: high-necked and long-sleeved. Her attitude toward home and family was anything but modern (higher education notwithstanding). Both Hayeses made every effort to provide a traditional White House, all the more so since the 1876 election was rancorous and disputed. Barely elected and tainted with the epithet "His Fraudulency," Hayes and his wife strove to remain personally above reproach.

Despite Lucy's sincere backseat temperament, she was hijacked twice. First, by Mary Clemmer Ames, a female reporter who proclaimed the First Lady to be the "New Woman." It is unclear exactly what characteristics Lucy had to warrant that claim other than a broad academic education. Nevertheless, Ames followed First Lady Hayes like a puppy dog, singing her New Woman praises. Lucy considered herself to be shy and denied being anything other than old-fashioned and a devoted family woman. But even after eight pregnancies, she was still attractive with a shapely albeit buxom figure. Compared to the homely Julia Grant and pouty-looking Mary Lincoln, Lucy was downright pretty.

Always a teetotaler by personal inclination, she had encouraged her husband to "take the pledge" early in their marriage. (The youthful Rutherford had been known to enjoy an occasional whiskey with his equally youthful companions.) The declaration that the White House would serve no wine, whiskey, or brandy became a cause célèbre, inviting more than a century of scholars to cast blame or praise wherever they chose. Did *Lucy* insist on the dry house? Or did *Rutherford* institute the policy as a popular issue to diffuse the questionable election and related political problems? Scholars have proposed different viewpoints. Lucy always claimed she was in favor of temperance rather than abstinence, and it was not in her character to impose her will on others. It may well be that her husband suggested that she take responsibility for the decision, since good manners would protect the First Lady from undue criticism (at least then). Besides, how could anyone condemn a first couple for opposing drunkenness? There will probably never be a definitive answer.

The dry dictum, however, was the impetus of Lucy's second hijacking, this time by the Women's Christian Temperance Union, an organization that was quickly becoming a formidable force in the country. Mostly comprised of prim, unappealing old biddies, the WCTU declared the First Lady to be their "ideal woman" and began singing an entire chorale of her praises from the rooftops. Their publications were continually filled with Lucy Hayes stories and tributes. She was embarrassed by the unsolicited publicity, but her lawyer husband advised her to let it slide unless people said something untrue or slanderous. Lucy herself never joined the WCTU either as First Lady or in her retirement. But she did accept the beautiful portrait of her they had commissioned.

One story that seems to have withstood scrutiny is how the devout Hayes family would invite selected guests to join them at the White House for coffee, cake, and hymn singing after church services on Sunday. The only people who criticized that benign ritual were the ribald politicians who remembered the less-pious, more-glamorous Grants with more affection than they had for Lemonade Lucy and her equally boring husband.

Postscript: LEGEND HAS IT THAT ORANGES, SECRETLY INJECTED WITH RUM, WERE PLENTIFUL IN THE ANTEROOMS OF THE HAYES WHITE HOUSE, WHERE THEY WERE IMMENSELY POPULAR. THERE IS AN AMENDED LEGEND THAT THE ORANGES WERE ONLY INJECTED WITH RUM FLAVORING. THIS WAS ANOTHER ONE OF THOSE "WAS IT LUCY OR RUTHERFORD WHO DICTATED DRY" PROPOSITIONS. WHATEVER IT WAS THAT CREATED SUCH A RUN ON ORANGES IS STILL UNKNOWN, BUT THE WHITE HOUSE WOULD NOT BE DRY AGAIN UNTIL PROHIBITION. AND "LEMONADE LUCY" WOULD STICK.

FRANCES CLEVELAND
1864–1947

FIRST LADY: 1886–89, 1893–97

A Star Is Born

When it was announced that the gruff, grumpy, overweight, forty-nine-year-old bachelor president was finally going to marry, the country was stunned and then delighted by his choice. Grover Cleveland would wed twenty-one-year-old Frances Folsom, recently graduated from Wells College. He had known her all her life. She was the daughter of his former law partner and close friend, Oscar Folsom. Cleveland had even presented the new parents with the baby carriage. When Folsom died nine years later, Cleveland, as estate executor, was named Frances's guardian and provided every advantage for the little girl and her widowed mother. Uncle Cleve would always be a prominent male figure for Frances as she grew up in Buffalo, New York.

About the time her hair went up and her hems came down, Democrat Grover Cleveland, then governor of New York, began looking at his ward with refocused interest. Their courtship, what little there was, was via letter and bouquet. But by the time he was inaugurated as president in 1885, he had proposed and she had accepted. Their engagement was a top presidential secret for more than a year while Frances and her mother traveled through Europe. Cleveland's bookish sister, Rose Elizabeth, grudgingly pinch-hit as White House hostess.

Cleveland's wedding in 1886 was the first time, and so far the only time, a sitting president was married in the White House. It had been one of the best-kept secrets of the day. People knew nothing about it until only a few days before the nuptials. Cleveland directed everything himself. He hand-wrote the fifty invitations, engaged the minister, and arranged the honeymoon. His sister planned the menu, ordered the flowers, and hired the Marine Band. All Frances and her mother had to do was buy gowns and show up. No press was invited. As a matter of fact, they were publicly and vociferously *excluded.*

There had not been a real First Lady in the White House for more than four years. James and Lucretia Garfield had very little time to make an impression. He was assassinated only three months into his term and spent another three months dying. Sophisticated New York widower Chester Alan Arthur installed his sister to do a few honors, but he preferred to do most of the honors himself. By the mid-1880s, the world was changing. Newspapers abounded, and women's magazines were flourishing. The "New Woman" proclaimed by Mary Clemmer Ames had actually taken hold, and for the first time in history, journalists were specifically assigned to report on the pretty, young, new First Lady's activities, starting with the wedding and the honeymoon. This galled President Cleveland to no end. He loathed intrusion into his personal life, possibly because of the scandal uncovered during his election campaign: he had fathered a child out of wedlock some twenty years earlier. He admitted it, documented his responsibility and financial contribution to the child's welfare, and the country obviously forgave him.

Cleveland may have disliked the press, but Frances would be its darling, and she never failed to charm them. She was a pretty girl, nearly five foot seven, with a good figure, an endearing smile, and dimples. The press adored her, and photographers did likewise. They always would. With her youthful vitality, she was the youngest First Lady ever, and she never objected to standing for hours to shake hands and say a few kind words to the thousands of people who lined up for her weekly receptions. During her first official hostess stint at the White House, a delighted Cleveland was seen to nudge his new mother-in-law and, grinning, say, "She'll do! She'll do!"

And Frances certainly did do. But she did only what Victorian convention and her superconventional husband permitted. He would no more think of consulting his wife about a political issue than he would consult a classroom of six-year-olds. She would do exactly what her husband wished, and she never "developed any notions," as Cleveland once remarked. "Frank" as he called her, would be the bouquet receiver, the smile bestower, the table arranger, the tea party hostess, and possibly an escort around town for occasional women's groups. In fact, the president so wanted to protect himself and *his wife* from the intrusion of the insatiable ghouls of the press, that he bought a private house for them in Georgetown and became a commuter.

But the letters came pouring in. Where previous First Ladies could count a few dozen unsolicited letters a week, Frances received hundreds. The White House would order ten thousand copies of her photograph only to reorder more in a few months. A form letter (hitherto considered discourteous) was devised to spare Frances from hours and hours of repetitious letter writing. And what were the letters about? Personal and usually trivial things. Things like what kind of hand cream she used, her perfume preference, or her favorite book, color, poem, or recipe. In the 1880s there was no law forbidding the unsanctioned use of a person's name or likeness in advertising, so Frances's pretty photo and implied endorsement was frequently seen praising the virtues of somebody's soaps and powders and pills. One manufacturer claimed that Mrs. Cleveland's peaches-and-cream complexion was due to her daily dose of their arsenic. The president righteously introduced legislation forbidding the use of photographs and endorsements without permission. It failed. Advertisers stepped up their campaigns. But while the grouchy Cleveland fumed, the First Lady continued to smile.

Frances's Legacy

Despite a notoriously grumpy and aging husband, despite no real romance in her young life, despite a lack of contemporaries and peer-companions, despite being sheltered and secluded, despite spending hours standing in receiving lines with forced smiles, despite hours spent answering unwanted and insipid letters, Frances never complained. She was **GOOD NATURED** about her duties, her husband, and life in general. It is not easy to maintain a pleasant disposition throughout the demands of First Ladydom, then or now. Frankie Cleveland's dimples and sweet temperament made her everyone's favorite for the rest of her long life.

Grover Cleveland was the only president to serve two non-consecutive terms, and by the time he was reelected in 1892, he and Frances were parents, with another baby on the way. The press returned in droves. Now the letters solicited her advice on child rearing. (She was only twenty-five!) People congregated outside the White House to get a glimpse of a nurse pushing the baby carriage. When one woman tried to snip a lock of the baby's hair, an incensed Cleveland took action. He had a fence built around the White House.

There are only two recorded instances of First Lady Frances taking a public or quasi-public position. When her husband wanted to go fishing one Sunday, she put her foot down, saying it wouldn't sit well for the president of the United States, and a minister's son at that, to dishonor the Sabbath. He reluctantly stayed home.

Then there is the story about Frances's receiving days, which drew literally thousands of well-wishers and tourists, happy to stand in line for hours just to shake her hand. One aide suggested she might change the date from her regular Saturday afternoons to cut down on the traffic. "But that's the only day that the shop-girls and government clerks can come," she explained. "Exactly," replied the sanctimonious aide. It is unknown if Frances ever thought that as a fatherless young woman herself, she might have become a shop-girl or clerk. What *is* known is that the Saturday afternoons remained.

For all their age and disposition differences, the Clevelands had a happy marriage—including five children. Friends said they parented each other as well. He doted on her like a favorite child, and she mothered him like one of their kids.

Postscript: FRANCES WAS THE FIRST FIRST LADY TO REMARRY. FIVE YEARS AFTER CLEVELAND DIED AT SEVENTY-ONE, AND WITH FOUR CHILDREN TO RAISE, SHE MARRIED PRINCETON PROFESSOR THOMAS PRESTON. SHE WAS MARRIED TO HIM FOR NEARLY THIRTY-FIVE YEARS, FIFTEEN LONGER THAN SHE WAS TO THE PRESIDENT—BUT SHE IS BURIED NEXT TO GROVER CLEVELAND.

CAROLINE HARRISON
1832–92

FIRST LADY: 1889–92

Alias Martha Stewart

Caroline Harrison is arguably one of the more obscure First Ladies who truly deserves far better recognition. She was active, vital, and gifted.

Born in Ohio to a minister-educator, Caroline Scott, called Carrie within the family, married her classmate Benjamin Harrison when she had just turned twenty-one. It would be a long financial struggle. Ben, a grandson of a president and a great-grandson of a wealthy Virginia signer of the Declaration of Independence, inherited little of their great estates, which had been long diluted by the large families of the early Harrisons.

Ben Harrison had studied the law, and in the days before the Civil War, young attorneys starting out were dependent on crumbs from their peers' tables. Having a reputation as a cold fish, Harrison received few referrals. But Carrie was a talented homemaker. She sewed, knitted, cooked, baked, gardened, canned, preserved, recycled, and reworked everything to make ends meet. She did it with so much style and taste that visitors to the newlyweds' little cabin would remark on how lovely it was. When their two children came along, she added mothering to her list.

Harrison augmented his meager income by serving as a court clerk, but even with that, he once considered giving up law entirely and buying a store so he could at least feed his family. At the start of the Civil War, Ben was thirty and decided to spend their life's savings to purchase a substitute to serve in his place, so his wife and two children would not be left unsupported. Fortunately for him, the governor of Indiana (where they then lived) was empowered to grant an officer's commission to any man who could raise a regiment. Harrison hung an American flag from his window with a sign that said "Enlist Here" and raised a regiment. The governor duly made him a colonel. Now at least he had an officer's pay to send home to Carrie. He eventually was promoted to brigadier general and served efficiently and honorably, mostly in an administrative capacity.

Administrative or not, brigadier generals and lawyers were prime political candidate material following the war (even better if they were Republicans), and Benjamin Harrison's star began to rise, wimpy handshake notwithstanding. His law practice began to flourish, and the Harrisons moved to a lovely house in a better section of Indianapolis. His political opinions were now actively sought, and he was sent to the Senate.

Carrie's Legacy

At a time when being a good housekeeper was considered the highest compliment a woman could receive, Caroline Harrison excelled in **HOUSEHOLD MANAGEMENT**. Even though she never had to wash a dish or polish a spoon in the White House, she knew exactly what needed to be done, and saw to it that the president's house not only ran smoothly, but positively sparkled. Nothing escaped her white glove. Today's White House employs a large professional housekeeping staff, but it still falls to the First Lady to oversee that department. Carrie was the best of the lot. By a lot.

With their two children nearly grown, Carrie could indulge her creative and artistic side: watercolors. She had always been an accomplished artist, and now she began china painting, a new and popular Victorian hobby. She installed a small kiln in her house and began giving classes to other women. She also played piano and organ, taught Sunday school, and was the president of the Indianapolis Woman's Club. And she still cooked and canned and gardened. She was one busy lady.

Harrison's path to become president was neither gradual nor meteoric, nor even merited. For more than a quarter century, presidential candidates were selected partly for geopolitical acceptability and partly because they were safe. They had incurred no strong opposition, nor were they likely to make political waves. Harrison fit the bill perfectly: Indiana was neither North nor South, and Ben was an administrator, not a wave maker. He was also the grandson of a former president, another asset. He was duly elected.

Carrie bustled into the White House and immediately took charge, eliminating waste and establishing order. Nearly sixty years old and fairly stout, she nevertheless rolled up her sleeves and made a complete and thorough inspection from attic to cellar and was dismayed at its condition. Termites, rats, and rot had done serious structural damage. Hoping to modernize and bring electricity to the White House in 1889 (it had been in other cities for more than a decade), they consulted Thomas Edison and his scientists, who spent two days poking around and declared that the mansion could not withstand the necessary wiring. It was a tinderbox. Besides being a firetrap with an outdated kitchen, Carrie also complained that there were insufficient rooms in the private quarters. The Harrisons had come to the White House with a large extended family: their two children, their spouses and their children, her aged father, her widowed sister, and her widowed niece. And there was only one bathroom! It was suggested that the

White House be torn down and a more suitable presidential palace be erected in its place, along the lines of its European counterparts. Architectural designs were solicited and a committee was formed, with Mrs. Harrison as a prominent member. But traditional heads prevailed, and Congress determined that the "Home of Jefferson and Lincoln" warranted repair not razing, and substantial renovations were made to support the necessary electrical wiring. But once there was light, the Harrison family refused to flip the switch on or off, fearful of electrocution.

Carrie also took a hand in modernizing the kitchens, which had not been updated for more than forty years. Next, she reorganized the conservatory (which stood where the West Wing is today), made sure that fresh flowers were displayed at all public functions, and generously dispatched bouquets to high-ranking government officials for births, bereavements, illness, and other notable events, "compliments of President and Mrs. Harrison."

Her china painting was not neglected either. If she received a letter announcing the birth of a baby named Benjamin, Caroline, or Harrison, a pink or blue baby cup, hand-painted by First Lady Harrison was promptly sent along with her best wishes. When she discovered parts of old dinner services used by past administrations collecting dust in the attic, she had them brought downstairs and carefully researched their place in history, thus beginning the famous Presidential China Collection that is a highlight of White House tours today.

Mrs. Harrison was also asked to serve as the first

president-general of the newly formed Daughters of the American Revolution. While she was not descended from the Virginia signer herself, her children were, and she was proud to lend her name and prestige. The DAR was happy to commission a suitable portrait.

In late 1891, Carrie began to weaken, and true to her bustling nature, she ignored it until it could no longer be ignored. She was diagnosed with "galloping consumption," a rapidly deteriorating form of tuberculosis, which then was always fatal. Within six months she was dead.

Postscript: MRS. HARRISON WAS NOT IMMUNE TO CARING ABOUT WOMEN'S ISSUES. WHEN JOHNS HOPKINS UNIVERSITY SOLICITED HER FOR A CONTRIBUTION TOWARD ITS NEW MEDICAL SCHOOL, CARRIE REPLIED THAT SHE WOULD BE HAPPY TO OBLIGE, PROVIDED THEY ACCEPTED WOMEN STUDENTS. THEY DID. SHE SENT HER DONATION. STOUT AND SIXTYISH OR NOT, SHE HAD THE REAL ELEMENTS OF THE NEW WOMAN.

EDITH ROOSEVELT
1861–1948

FIRST LADY: 1901–09

The Elegant White House

There was never a time Edith Carow did not know Theodore Roosevelt. Her best friend Corinne was Theodore's younger sister, and their nannies wheeled their prams around Gramercy Park in New York City. Hers was an old and decent family, but her father was inclined toward drink and thus a spotty provider. The kindly patrician Roosevelts included little Edie in their outings whenever possible. Most of their acquaintances believed that when the children grew up, Edith would marry Theodore. But it didn't happen. At least not the way they thought.

Theodore went off to college and fell deeply in love with beautiful and wealthy Alice Lee. They married when Theodore graduated. True to her steely reserved nature, Edith Carow showed little outward regret and kicked up her heels at the wedding. What happened within Edith usually stayed within Edith. Since her family's lack of finances precluded either a college education or a traditional social debut, and it would have been social suicide to get a job, she led a quiet life, seeing a few friends, reading voraciously, and keeping to herself. She seemed destined to become an old maid.

Three years later, Theodore's young wife died in childbirth. The grieving husband deposited his infant daughter with his *older* sister and went west to become a cowboy. It would be another two years until Theodore and Edith became reacquainted. This time, the grown man and the attractive twenty-five-year-old young woman discovered the commonalities that would make for a happy, prosperous, and never-boring union.

First and foremost, according to those who knew her, Edith Roosevelt was a wife and mother. In addition to baby Alice, there would be five more vigorous Roosevelts, all possessed of their father's abundant energy and vitality and both parents' unending curiosity about everything. It is said that Theodore read a book a day, and Edith matched him one-for-one, albeit their tastes were different. His were more scientific, hers more arty. What developed was an incredibly broad range of subjects that could and would be discussed intelligently and in detail at their always-lively dinner table. Since Theodore Roosevelt was not only wide-ranging and political, but very,

very social, their large family table was usually expanded to include numerous, diverse guests nearly every night.

Edith R.'s Legacy

When Edith Roosevelt was First Lady, it was as if the stars had aligned themselves in a smiley face over the White House. The country was at peace. It was prospering at a rapid rate. Her family enjoyed vigorous good health. She was completely equal to and comfortable with the tasks set before her. She was constantly surrounded by the most fascinating people. She was married to a man who was devoted to her, the man she had loved since childhood. And he was hugely popular! Edith was **HAPPY and LUCKY**, perhaps more a wish than a legacy. And nobody gets better than that!

While Edith was as bright and intelligent as one would expect of a Roosevelt mate, her temperament was cooler; many said cold. She seldom lost her temper, but her distance and verbal antipathy could be venomous. Her daughter once said, "Mother took no prisoners." It would fall to Edith to manage the household, the servants, the children, the money, and Theodore. It was not an easy task. He indulged himself with yearly six-week hunting vacations out west, leaving his wife to entertain, amuse, supervise, and move the children back and forth between their Washington residence and their New York home on Long Island. If she ever objected, it was private. Perhaps she considered it her great blessing to finally marry the man she had always loved.

TR, like Thomas Jefferson, was a man of many careers all practiced simultaneously, but never in a way to amass a fortune. First and foremost, he was a Republican politician. Then came amateur natural scientist, ranch owner, and prolific writer. By forty, he had secured a spot as assistant secretary of the navy under President William McKinley, single-handedly (according to his critics) fomented the Spanish-American War, resigned to command the volunteer Rough Rider regiment, charged up San Juan Hill to become a hero, then became governor of New York, vice president, and finally president—all within three years. It was par for the course. Edith, of course, took it in stride, as she took everything.

Only forty when she entered the White House after McKinley's assassination, Edith Roosevelt's contribution to the realm of First Ladyhood had much in common with that of Jacqueline Kennedy a half century later: class and elegance. The repairs and refurbishing undertaken under Caroline Harrison only a decade earlier proved to be inadequate, considering the new inventions and technologies pouring out of the Patent Office. The return of the second Cleveland administration had contributed little in redecoration, and frail Ida McKinley undertook no projects. The Roosevelts, however, would make huge alterations. The White House needed to expand with the new century.

Even with the Harrison expansion, the private family quarters were insufficient for Theodore, Edith, six children, a menagerie of pets, frequent guests, plus presidential office space. The downstairs area was strictly for formal and ceremonial entertaining. So Caroline Harrison's beloved conservatory was demolished and replaced by the West Wing. That would be Theodore's domain. Edith took charge of much of the mansion's transition into the twentieth century, and it would now officially be called the White House on the letterhead. The large East Room was stripped of its hotel lobby décor and painted white and gold. The full-length portraits of George and Martha Washington were removed from other locations and hung on each side of the fireplace. The room today is very much the same as it was when Edith redecorated. The Roosevelts also wanted to make the White House look like home, so the dining room sported elk and moose trophies.

Parties were elegant but not lavish. Edith was a thrifty woman, and entertainment expenses were still out of the president's pocket. The guest list, however, was always a who's who of the finest talents and intellects in the world. Their contemporaries said that Theodore and Edith Roosevelt's gatherings were more like a cultural salon than the center of political society.

In her own way, Edith seemed to have a sixth sense for protocol and appropriate etiquette, and she watched her over-exuberant husband like a hawk. Even though she kept to the background, one look, or her cautionary, "Now, Theodore," and the contrite president would immediately cease whatever he was doing that gave her pause.

Her admirers said that Edith Roosevelt was the only First Lady who never made a mistake. Perhaps so, but her mark as First Lady, classy or not, leaves no real fingerprint. In part, she was overshadowed by a husband whose fingers were on everything. Then, too, there would be another Mrs. Roosevelt who would leave indelible fingerprints. Edith's detractors claimed she seemed cocooned within her own hard, private shell that few were ever able to crack. Theodore could crack that shell of course. But he died prematurely at sixty, and she outlived him by nearly thirty years.

No one else seems to have cracked that shell.

Postscript: EDITH NEVER HUNTED MOOSE OR BIG GAME OR EXPLORED UNCHARTED RIVERS, BUT SHE THOROUGHLY ENJOYED INSPECTING ALL THE COLLECTIONS OF ROCKS, INSECTS, PLANTS, AND ANIMALS LARGE AND SMALL THAT FOUND THEIR WAY TO SAGAMORE HILL. SHE CLIMBED AND HIKED, SWAM, RODE, AND ROWED AND WAS HAPPY TO PARTICIPATE IN WHATEVER WAS ESSENTIAL TO ROOSEVELTIAN FUN. ONE SON SAID, "WHEN MOTHER WAS A LITTLE GIRL, SHE MUST HAVE BEEN A LITTLE BOY."

NELLIE TAFT
1861–1943

FIRST LADY: 1909–13

The Wind Beneath

There was nothing shy, retiring, domestic, or deferential about Helen Herron, called Nellie from birth. Born to a prominent Cincinnati, Ohio, family at the outset of the Civil War, Nellie would rail internally against the Victorian constrictions of the feminine world. She clandestinely smoked cigarettes, drank whiskey, and gambled at cards by the time she was fifteen—habits she kept all her life.

At sixteen she spent a week at the White House, a guest of President and Mrs. Rutherford B. Hayes, who were close family friends. From that moment on, Nellie's overwhelming goal was to occupy that same residence as Mrs. First Resident herself. The only path open for an ambitious woman at that time was via a promising spouse. William Howard Taft, who she married when she was twenty-five, had that promise. Besides boasting a Cincinnati pedigree surpassing the Herrons, Will had graduated at the top of his class at Yale, and at three hundred pounds, he was a huge mountain of lovable fellow who adored his sometimes witty and frequently sharp-tongued wife. Republican doors swung open for him.

The biggest threat to Nellie's presidential ambitions was that Will didn't share them. His ambitions pointed a mile down Pennsylvania Avenue in the other direction: the Supreme Court. Will was a jurist by temperament and inclination, as he would be for the rest of his life. Nellie believed that same temperament and inclination would serve just as effectively in the executive branch. More important, she believed the executive branch would suit *her* temperament and inclination much better than the stuffy old court.

So she joined, participated in, subscribed to, supported, and contributed to everything that would further her goal. As keeper of the family purse, she made sure political obligations were paid first. The tight-knit and well-moneyed Taft brothers were also inclined to agree with Nellie's viewpoint, and they willingly gave her an important seat at the family council table. With their support and her inherent thrift, finances or lack thereof would never be a serious problem.

Nellie was a Gemini, however, and the mischievous twins of her stars would play havoc within her own nature. Always a tightly wound perfectionist, she could make a half dozen fine decisions during the day only to toss and turn all night second-guessing herself and worrying everything to death.

Nellie's Legacy

Nellie Taft is a big what-if. In only three months she would break numerous precedents and likely would have broken more if her health had permitted. She had **AMBITION** of both kinds—the ambition to want something and the ambition to work for it. Will Taft would have never been president if Nellie hadn't been standing behind him with a cattle prod. No one gets very far without ambition, and Nellie had more of it than any of her predecessors. Maybe even more than her successors too.

In 1899, right after the Spanish-American War, the Philippine Islands fell generally unwanted into our lap. The islands were steeped in generations of chaotic religious and political factions, and President McKinley wisely appointed Taft, a man of good will and excellent jurisprudence, to serve as governor-general. Nellie, who loved exotic travel almost as much as political power, was delighted to move to the islands with three children in tow. They would be her happiest years, although she didn't know it at the time. There, ensconced in Manila's beautiful Malacañan Palace, she was the first lady of the Philippines in a dress rehearsal for her plans for Washington. She entertained lavishly, mixing her nonprejudicial attitudes with elegance and etiquette. She undertook a program to provide milk to indigent Filipino children. She also managed to indulge her tastes for adventure and rode in war canoes, trekked muleback into the Luzon jungles "where no white woman had ever gone before," and even took a solo side trip to Japan. Meanwhile, Taft was sincerely endearing himself to the Filipino people and actually establishing order.

After the anguish of declining two offers of a Supreme Court appointment because of his commitments in the Philippines, Will finally received the one he couldn't refuse: secretary of war under his good friend President Theodore Roosevelt. Nellie was thrilled. It was the opportunity she had been waiting for. It was an important cabinet post and visibly placed on the path to the White House itself.

With the country at peace, the secretary of war had little to do except serve as TR's troubleshooter, a job well suited to Taft's talents. His star was rising. TR had also made a promise not to seek a second term (which he regretted the moment he uttered it) and needed to groom a successor. Theodore wanted Taft to run. So did Nellie. So did the Brothers Taft. The only one waffling was Will Taft himself, but he was outnumbered. So he ran and won.

Nellie's dream had come true. Since Taft now had a hefty $75,000 annual salary, he insisted that she indulge herself with a luscious new wardrobe. The glamorous Edwardian styles of the day were particularly becoming to the forty-eight-year-old woman with a good figure. At her insistence, she rode in the car beside the newly elected president—the first First Lady to ride with her husband. (Incoming and outgoing First Ladies previously rode together.) She began to redecorate and rearrange the furniture, which included removing the Roosevelt trophy heads. She contracted with the Cadillac Company to provide two automobiles gratis for presidential use in return for the privilege of saying so (didn't everyone in Europe?); integrated the staff dining room over many objections; and turned a large section of the Tidal Basin area into a pedestrian park with free band concerts for everyone. The emperor of Japan, remembering Mrs. Taft from her earlier visit, sent hundreds of cherry seedlings to enhance the promenade. True to her nervous nature, Nellie fretted that no one would attend the first concert, but more than ten thousand people showed up.

The Greek definition of tragedy is based on great height preceding great fall. The gods had granted Nellie's wish. The goal had been reached. But a few months later, the gods turned. Nellie collapsed from a severe stroke. While she was not physically paralyzed, she suffered from aphasia and some facial disfiguring. In short, Nellie Taft could not communicate or be seen in public. She knew and understood everything that was going on, but her speech was garbled and her face contorted. She could not read or write. She could no longer be a participant. She could not even share her thoughts with her husband. It would take nearly the rest of Will Taft's term for her to regain these lost abilities. Still, she worked behind the scenes as much as possible, planning guest lists and menus and table arrangements and whatever she could do without undue stress. Her health was her main focus from that point on.

One aide painted a heart-wrenching scene: a magnificent state banquet that Nellie had helped to plan but could not attend. Instead, bejeweled and dressed to the teeth in one of her elegant gowns, she sat alone at a table in an adjoining room, eating party food, and listening at a door left slightly ajar so she could hear what went on.

All the great plans she had envisioned as First Lady, all the programs and good works she hoped to espouse, all the grand entertainment she had seen in her mind's eye, and perhaps even her lasting place in the pantheon of First Ladies, all were gone in a moment's collapse.

Nellie recovered, although her speech would always be somewhat slurred. But what she had lost was her hard drive. Even though she lived past eighty, and even though she always maintained a lively interest in the political scene, and even though her husband became chief justice of the Supreme Court in his postpresidential career, Nellie's greatest task was to quiet her restless soul. When she wrote her memoirs, she focused on the Philippines. The White House chapters were merely lists of guests and table decorations. If she grieved for her lost dreams, it was private.

Postscript: THE TAFT FAMILY TODAY, TO THE FIFTH AND SIXTH GENERATION, LOOMS LARGE AND RESPECTED IN OHIO AND EVEN NATIONAL POLITICS. NELLIE IS THEIR MATRIARCH.

ELLEN WILSON
1860–1914

FIRST LADY: 1913–14

The Steel Magnolia

When Ellen Axson was twenty, her mother died, leaving her to care for her brothers, ages fourteen and four, and the infant sister whose birth contributed to her mother's early death. Then there was her father, a Presbyterian minister who battled crippling depression all his life and would succumb not long thereafter.

Born in Savannah, Georgia, just as the Civil War commenced, Ellen had known little luxury. Ministers are seldom wealthy, and the decimated South could barely provide for its clergy. After a conventional education, Ellen had hoped to teach art, for which she had a decided talent. Her mother's death ended that dream, however. Her only goal became keeping her family together.

When she married Woodrow Wilson after an ardent two-year courtship mostly by correspondence, she was twenty-five. He was a twenty-eight-year-old scholar, just starting his academic career. Agreeing from the beginning to provide a home for Ellen's brothers, the new couple would never know an empty house. Their three daughters came in rapid succession in the first five years. There was also a revolving door of Woodrows, Wilsons, and Axsons as long-term houseguests. With so many mouths to feed, Professor Wilson, whose academic stature would soar from the start, began augmenting his insufficient salary with extra lectures and seminars and also churned out a book nearly every year. The stress, along with his personal need for constant perfection and emotional reassurance, would take its toll: his always-delicate health suffered, which included two mis- or undiagnosed strokes before he was forty.

It would fall to Ellen to be the earth mother and soother of wounds. She was the adhesive to hold the family, the house, the finances, and Woodrow together. She managed to do it all in her quiet and gentle way, which included becoming an intelligent audience for her brilliant husband. From the beginning of their courtship, Woodrow treated her as an intellectual equal, writing to her as he might write an academic colleague. He never gave a lecture series or submitted a manuscript without her preview and input. Woodrow the professor was a superb teacher. Ellen would always ask pithy and insightful questions. Her comments were always considered.

Ellen also knew intuitively that she lacked the sophistication for the witty dinner table banter that her husband so loved. Instead, whenever his programs took him to other universities, she encouraged him to participate as a single and charm all the worldly wives and daughters of his academic associates. She supported his separate vacations where he could relieve those tensions that always bubbled like simmering magma within. She firmly believed that she had bartered frivolous cosmopolitan pleasures for something far better. She also knew Woodrow's love for her ran deep and true and had no doubt that she was married to the most wonderful man in the world. They would write each other loving letters every day they were apart—even decades after their marriage.

By the time Wilson was a serious presidential contender, he had spent two decades shepherding Princeton to become one of the most academically prestigious colleges in the country. Considered a safe, conservative Democratic candidate, he was easily elected governor of New Jersey. Meanwhile, Ellen had become a capable hostess, business manager, political confidante, and watchful observer of Woodrow's precarious health. She also had the innate tact and savvy to run surreptitious interference for the turbulent personal-professional relationships that seemed to be a part of her husband's personality. Also, by the time Wilson was a serious contender, their daughters were grown. Ellen now had some uncrowded hours to unpack brushes and paints and devote more time to herself and her art. Hers was a serious talent, far more developed than Caroline Harrison's gift for china painting.

Even before she had First Lady notoriety, she had earned the respect and regard of several important American impressionists of the early twentieth century. She sold. She submitted. She competed. She won prizes.

Ellen's Legacy

Ellen Wilson, in her own unassuming way, had a **GENEROSITY OF SOUL** that is hard to equal. Everyone else's interest came before her own, and she offered it gladly. Other First Ladies would be generous with their time, talents, support, and even money, but Ellen's bounty would penetrate to her core. Even in dying, she placed her husband's responsibilities as president before her own health or need for personal comfort. On her deathbed, she gave Woodrow Wilson "permission," as it were, to love again without guilt. When he remarried, he would always know it was with Ellen's blessing.

Two years later, Wilson was elected president. Ellen believed with all her heart that he was the best qualified person to run the country, and whether she wanted it or not (and she said she didn't), being First Lady was part of the bargain. Her tenure would only last fifteen months, but in that time she made two notable contributions. The first is the Rose Garden that exists to this day. She had noticed the spot the day of Wilson's inauguration, and her artist's eye could see its potential. She worked closely with the White House gardeners to plan it, although she would not live to see its full glory.

Her second contribution is frequently and unjustly poohpoohed by subsequent historians who measure against the present and demand executive foresight and skills from First Ladies who barely understood that concept. Within walking distance of the 1913 White House was a foul slum of shanties built as temporary housing for former slaves after the Civil War. They were ugly, fetid, unsanitary, and bred disease. Ellen and several congressional wives mounted an intense lobbying campaign to have the eyesore removed. This would mark the first time a First Lady had undertaken a serious nondomestic public role. Others, of course, would follow, but she was the first. With little precedent to guide them since social activism was still in its infancy, little attention if any was given to the consequent problems of the displaced residents. "Mrs. Wilson's Bill," as it was called, was doubtlessly naive in a way, but had she lived, it is likely that she would have continued her involvement and advocacy to the next steps.

But Ellen came to the White House with a secret—one she didn't even know herself. Her health was failing. She blamed her flagging energy on the fact that she was fifty-four years old and had undertaken an enormous social schedule, including planning a grand White House wedding for her daughter. A year into Wilson's presidency, she had a fall. While it did not cause serious injury, it was a shock to her system and required medical attention. When she did not respond adequately to the prescribed treatment, Dr. Cary Grayson, their personal physician who had become a close friend to both Wilsons, decided to look further. It did not take long for him to discover the alarming symptoms of Bright's disease, a kidney ailment, then always fatal. She had had it for years.

Ellen and her doctor decided to withhold that information from the president until such time as it no longer could be concealed. Woodrow had enough stress dealing with accelerating hostilities in Europe. He was only told the inevitable two days before his wife died, just as the guns of August were booming their way into World War I.

Postscript: SHORTLY BEFORE HER DEATH, ELLEN CONFIDED TO DR. GRAYSON THAT IT WOULD BE HER WISH THAT WOODROW REMARRY IF THE OPPORTUNITY AROSE. SHE KNEW BETTER THAN ANYONE HOW MUCH HE NEEDED A WOMAN'S SUPPORT AND COMFORTING PRESENCE IN HIS LIFE. IT WAS THE GREATEST GIFT SHE WOULD GIVE HIM.

EDITH WILSON
1872–1961

FIRST LADY: 1915–21

~~~~◦◦~~~~

Dragon Lady

Woodrow Wilson was practically paralyzed with grief when Ellen died, but less than a year later, that grief would be replaced by euphoria.

Edith Bolling was born into an old (dating to Pocahontas), genteel Virginia family (her father was a judge) not long after the Civil War had left everything in ruins. As the seventh of nine children and a girl to boot, there was little left for Edith's education except the admonition to marry well and provide for herself. She did. At twenty-four, after a four-year tepid courtship, she married Norman Galt, a prestigious

Washington jeweler a dozen years her senior. Their marriage, albeit childless, was pleasant enough. When he died a decade later, Edith was his sole heir. She would never need to worry about money.

She met Woodrow Wilson by chance, having been invited for tea at the White House by Helen Bones, the president's cousin who had come to assume social and house-management duties after Ellen's death. Woodrow's reaction to the attractive forty-two-year-old widow was instantaneous and fervent. "Cousin Helen's friend" was invited to lunches, teas, private suppers, and afternoon drives, and it did not take very long for Edith to realize she was being wooed. Daily letters passed between them. The president had a private phone line installed between the White House and her town house only a mile away. He was a passionate and romantic courtier. Edith, whose courtship by Norman Galt did not include passionate wooing, was overwhelmed. The fact that it had been less than a year since his wife had died mattered little to the president. He was in love, and the Widow Galt had become the center of his life. Acutely aware of conventional mourning practice, Edith offered to wait. Woodrow, who could not bear to be thwarted, wouldn't hear of it. They were married only fifteen months after Ellen's funeral.

Far from being outraged or shocked by Wilson's early remarriage, the country was genuinely happy for him. So were the Wilson daughters and other kin. The president and his ladylove were seen together all the time. Edith, statuesque at five feet nine, presented a formidable picture, usually photographed wearing a big cartwheel hat and a ubiquitous orchid corsage. They would have the one thing that had been lacking in Wilson's first marriage: the luxury of time and companionship. With no family responsibilities along with secure finances, the newlyweds became inseparable.

Edith W.'s Legacy

Edith Wilson, at five feet nine, would only be equaled physically by Lou Hoover, Eleanor Roosevelt, and Michelle Obama. Standing nose-to-nose with most of the political figures of her era, she presented an intimidating sense of **COMMAND**, and the good manners of that day had men politely deferring to the fair sex whether they liked it or not. Other First Ladies might employ tact or subtlety, but Edith was neither tactful nor subtle. She commanded attention and regard. If she didn't like you, she never minced words. And if you didn't like her either, too bad.

Dr. Cary Grayson had confided Woodrow's delicate health conditions to the new Mrs. W., stressing the importance of rest and relaxation in the president's schedule. She took the charge seriously. She watched over his diet, and they began playing nine holes of golf together early every morning. Neither were good golfers, but the fresh air and exercise was exactly what was needed. And they had fun. She was also a shrewd financial manager, and Woodrow was relieved to have her handle the family funds, just as Ellen had done.

Meanwhile, Woodrow the professor had begun to educate his bride. He had a desk for her moved into his private office, and he began discussing complex issues in serious depth, along with perspicacious analyses of the current politicians. He fully expected she would understand. Edith, like Ellen, was an apt student. She also began reading her way through his library and learned quickly, although several key aides were taken aback by how familiar the new Mrs. Wilson was with political matters, including some that were top secret. They were also miffed at her tendency to insert comments during high-level discussions. At the time, nobody had an inkling that she was being groomed for a subsequent role.

Her popularity at first was solid, especially when she allowed herself to be photographed in a Red Cross hat and apron, helping with the war effort. That one photo was said to have inspired thousands of women to volunteer. But the Great War, hard fought and hard won, proved much easier than winning the peace.

Against all political advice, the idealistic Wilson decided to cross the Atlantic to lead the American peace commission personally. His popularity soared abroad, but the wily old European politicians cared little about peace, let alone ideals, and focused only on reparations and grand-scale land grabs. Wilson was no match. He gave way on nearly every issue to save his greatest dream: a League of Nations. The League, he convinced himself, would mean an end to all wars. His popularity began to sour and then decline precipitously at home. The stress of the overseas negotiations plus a balky Congress in Washington led to a massive stroke.

In fairness to Edith, whose popularity would plummet, it was primarily the medical community that dictated the ensuing events. All Wilson's doctors (and there were several) agreed a) he would live; b) his chances for substantial recovery were excellent; c) there were no signs of long term mental decline or aphasia; and most importantly, d) it was essential to his recovery that Wilson retain the aura of being in control as president. To relinquish responsibility to the vice president would destroy his will to live. (There was also no real mechanism in place for a transfer of power, which would create a constitutional crisis.) The doctors were correct on all counts. Wilson lived for another five years, and while he would be frail and never walk again without two canes, he did make substantial improvement. What they failed to recognize at the time was his noticeable personality change. Always inclined toward self-righteousness and stubbornness, he now became generally paranoid and intransigent.

Edith, who had become the only one that Woodrow completely trusted, was now the gatekeeper. She would refer to it as her stewardship. The one time she had the temerity to suggest that he might compromise on a minor point, he said piteously, "Don't you turn on me too, Little Girl. I couldn't bear it." She was devastated. She never did it again.

Still a newlywed, her only concern was the well-being of Woodrow, her ailing husband. Woodrow the ailing president was far down on the list. He needed rest; she saw that he got it. He could only work an hour or two a day. The doctors suggested that she review all Wilson's correspondence first, so she read and summarized all communications, determined what was most important, and brought them to his attention. Most importantly, Woodrow needed to avoid stressful, unpleasant, or adversarial confrontation. Edith guarded that door like a ferocious watchdog, keeping the politicians at bay. His advisors, cabinet members, and congressional leaders of both parties unanimously resented the "undue influence" of the second Mrs. Wilson, who obstructed their access to the ailing president. But according to her own memoirs, she made no presidential or policy decisions, doing only and exactly what Woodrow entrusted or instructed her to do. She said he asked thousands of questions, insisted on knowing every detail, and told her which senators to send for and what suggestions he would make to them. She claimed that she made copious notes of everything "to be sure there were no mistakes." Woodrow Wilson was still running the show, although few realized it.

Edith Wilson was not a particularly tactful or likable person. She had definite opinions and was never shy about expressing them. She never forgave a slight. Woodrow's adversaries were her own. He once called her a "good hater." Her formidable presence, terminating meetings that ran too long, or placing a cautionary finger to her lips if the subject was touchy, angered the politicians who were quick to cry "Petticoat Government!" As Wilson's intransigence and paranoia increased and his physical strength ebbed, it would be the second Mrs. Wilson who received their undisguised annoyance and resentment for barring the door.

Edith outlived Woodrow Wilson by more than thirty-five years, devoting herself to perpetuating his memory and accomplishments and accepting bouquets from League of Nations officialdom, which never included American membership. She also outlived and alienated everyone associated with the Wilson era, including his three daughters.

Postscript: PEOPLE LOVE TO REFER TO EDITH WILSON AS OUR FIRST FEMALE PRESIDENT. SHE NEVER THOUGHT SO OR VIEWED HERSELF AS SUCH, NOR DID SHE APPRECIATE THE ALLUSION. AND, COME TO THINK OF IT, THE STATEMENT IS NEVER MADE IN ADMIRATION—NOT EVEN BY HER ADMIRERS. IT IS ALWAYS A HOSTILE REMARK.

FLORENCE HARDING
1860–1924

FIRST LADY: 1921–23

Duchess

Florence Kling was the daughter of the wealthiest—and nastiest—man in Marion, Ohio. He ruled his family with an iron fist, and his headstrong daughter, more like him than she perhaps cared to admit, rebelled. At eighteen, she took up with Henry DeWolfe, the town bad boy, who even then had a reputation for hard drinking. They eloped once she found herself pregnant. Within three years, he deserted her and their baby, leaving them penniless. She crept back to Marion with her head high, took a cheap room at a cheap boardinghouse, and tried to support herself and the child by giving piano lessons. They barely made ends meet. Her father then made a devil's bargain with her: he would raise the boy as his own, provided Florence relinquish all parental rights. If she suffered over the decision, it is unrecorded. Her maternal instinct was never that strong, and now she was able to live her own life.

Not long after she divorced DeWolfe (who subsequently died), she met Warren Harding. Five years her junior, he had purchased a small interest in the *Marion Star,* a floundering weekly newspaper, and came to town to drum up business. Good looking, good natured with a born "hail fellow well met" personality, Warren quickly made friends in town. He eventually met Florence, who was immediately smitten. She was undeniably the pursuer in the relationship, and for whatever reasons (pregnancy not being one of them), he married her. He was twenty-five, she thirty.

Within the first ten years of their marriage, three important events occurred. First, Florence developed a serious and chronic kidney condition that would keep her bedridden for weeks and sometimes months at a time. More than once, her death was expected. Second, and as a direct result of her illness, the marital side of their marriage was curtailed. They would share a room but not a bed, and they would have no children together. Still young, handsome, and virile, Warren would find his pleasures elsewhere. There would be *many* elsewheres, usually with the "sporting" kind of women who were not averse to publicizing the liaison for their own gain. Florence invariably would find out, and there would be mega-rows. The marriage was far from happy, yet there is no record that either of them ever pressed for a divorce.

Third, the *Marion Star* began to thrive. Once when Warren was sick at home, he asked Florence to go to the office and fetch some paperwork. She discovered the place in a shambles and set about putting it in order. Having no children, few friends, a good business head, and time on her hands, she stayed for fourteen years, carving a place for herself in the circulation department. With his wife capably handling much of the newspaper's business, Harding continued his pleasurable "elsewheres." He was also free to pursue his growing interest in civic affairs and politics. He became a frequent guest speaker at various organizations and discovered a knack for the florid oratory of the time, "bloviating" as he called it, about the traditional platitudes: mom, apple pie, home, country, and Republican issues. Florence, who he had begun to call "Duchess" for her imperious and bossy manner, gravitated to politics like a cat to cream. She had shrewd instincts and a sensitive finger on the public pulse. The political wannabes who had begun to cling to Harding because "he looked like a man who should be president" put up with the Duchess at first. Then the Ohio Gang, as they were later called, began to respect her opinions. Eventually they realized that she was absolutely essential to any plans they might have for Warren Harding. He had only mild ambition for political advancement. It would always fall to the Duchess to swing for the bleachers.

In 1914, Warren was elected to the U.S. Senate, where

once again he slipped effortlessly into that good old boys club of like-minded congressmen who enjoyed whiskey, cards, and floozies. The Duchess, however, who had hoped to have a fresh start in Washington, was lonelier than ever. Now in her midfifties, she was considered old, dowdy, and socially outré. Her calls went unreturned; she was seldom invited anywhere. On top of everything, she had another severe bout of kidney trouble. Finally she received a great gift. She met Evalyn Walsh McLean, a wealthy, cosmopolitan socialite twenty years her junior who had married a man even wealthier than she. Ned McLean owned the *Washington Post* and the Hope Diamond. Their friendship was instantaneous and sincere. Under Evalyn's guidance, Florence bought fashionable clothes, went to fashionable parties, participated in fashionable causes, and had a second home at the McLeans' opulent and fashionable estate. Since Ned McLean's personal predilections were as raunchy as Harding's, the friendship was cemented all the way around. It was Evalyn who introduced the Duchess to Madame Marcia, a fashionable Washington fortune-teller who predicted that Warren Harding would be president but would not survive his term.

How and why Harding became president in the election of 1920 is a long and complicated story. He was personally ambivalent, content to be reelected to the Senate, and considered a shoo-in. He was also acutely aware of his lack of qualifications. Always superstitious, Florence had faith in Madame Marcia. She pressed hard to keep him in the race. The election of 1920 was the first in which women could vote, and handsome Warren, who truly looked presidential, won in a walk. First Lady Duchess, now past sixty, with years of chronic illness coupled with a genetic disposition to wrinkle despite every effort to remain youthful, looked like his mother.

Florence's Legacy

Florence Harding had the **GRIT TO SURVIVE**. She survived her despotic father, a failed first marriage to a drunk, a turbulent second marriage to a serial philanderer, a lonely and generally friendless existence, poor health, and the knowledge that their house of cards would crumble. If her health hadn't failed, she probably would have survived that too. Nothing ever stopped her from holding her head high and pressing onward. The Duchess was one tough cookie.

More than anything, Harding wanted to be a beloved president. He assumed that if he appointed good men to key positions, he could successfully be the face of the presidency, greeting, glad-handing, and exuding official charm, all of which he did splendidly. For her part, the Duchess wanted to be accessible, privately scorning the pretentious and supercilious manners of the last two decades of her predecessors. One of her first acts was to host an enormous garden party for wounded veterans. VA hospitals around the capital were emptied, and hundreds of soldiers came for sandwiches, cake, and lemonade. It was a beautiful spring day, perhaps the happiest day she would ever know. She also continued to be politically active behind the scenes, reading every speech before her husband made them and putting her two cents in. Warren usually listened. His wife was a shrewd woman.

Harding's appointments turned out to be a mixed bag. Some were very, very good, but like the little girl with a curl, some were horrid. It would take more than two years before there were undercurrents that all was not right in his official family. While Harding was inadequate in many ways, he was basically an honest man, but he was a dreadful judge of character when it came to his buddies. For all her political savvy, Florence had the same naiveté. Both Hardings were loyal by nature, and it was a crushing blow for them to learn, gradually at first, and then in an avalanche, that their dear friends were no more than common criminals, into the public till up to their elbows—all on Harding's watch.

His nerves shot, his stomach tormented, unable to sleep, with a heart condition that had been misdiagnosed for years, Harding had a massive coronary that killed him instantly. The Duchess would burn most of his papers and survive him by only a year.

Postscript: As an aging and ailing widow, the Duchess received a final humiliation. It seems that her philandering husband had fathered an illegitimate child shortly before his nomination in 1920. The new mother, like so many of his previous chippies, wanted money. Florence adamantly refused. She went to her grave disbelieving that latest episode. But like all the others, that one was true too.

GRACE COOLIDGE
1879–1957

FIRST LADY: 1923–29

Bountiful Graces

When Calvin Coolidge introduced Grace Goodhue to his family, they called her a likely gal and advised him to marry her. It was a different story for the Goodhues. The middle-class New Englanders loved their only daughter and wanted her to be happy. She was pretty, educated at the University of Vermont, and a teacher of the deaf. She was also outgoing and winsome. She could have had her pick. What could she possibly see in the mediocre, pasty cold clam who never said more than six words at a time?

But marry they did, and they were surprisingly happy. She

was twenty-six, he thirty-three. Calvin was indisputably the breadwinner and, in today's world, undeniably sexist. Grace was the bread baker, undeniably domestic. Both would be ordinary, but they were content in their respective spheres. Grace was happy being Mrs. Coolidge, housewife. She raised two sons, cooked, cleaned, knitted and crocheted, joined the Red Cross, volunteered at their church, took long morning constitutionals for exercise, and socialized with dozens of friends. Most of the time, she was unaware of the middling political activities of her other half. In fact, when Coolidge became lieutenant governor of Massachusetts, Grace didn't even know he had been running.

What she did know, however, was that Calvin loved her dearly in his own undemonstrative and understated way. His Yankee sense of thrift was legendary. They would live in half of a rented two-family house until after he retired from the presidency. Their silverware had a monogrammed *N* on it, bought when the Norwood Hotel closed. Since knives and forks don't wear out, they never saw fit to buy others. His only extravagance was reserved for Grace. He insisted that his wife have a stylish and expensive wardrobe, and he personally chose most of her hats. They both had a sense of humor that complemented each other. Hers, overt and mimicking; his, wry and deadpanned. And they were both incorrigible teases.

By the mid-nineteen-teens, social politics were beginning to emerge from stag-only affairs. Wives frequently were included. Coolidge had a pretty, stylish, personable wife with a wall-to-wall smile. She mixed easily into society, offsetting her obviously uncomfortable and uncommunicative husband. She could chat happily about the latest vaudeville acts or movies or novels—and baseball, which she loved. Everybody remembered the delightful Mrs. Coolidge. Former President Taft commented that marrying Grace was the best political decision Coolidge ever made.

Grace's Legacy

None of the old First Ladies have gone down in history as being a barrel of laughs, but Grace Coolidge is the only one whose **SENSE OF HUMOR** has been noted time and again. Her broad grin became a spontaneous laugh. She was said to have a gift of mimicry and could imitate her husband's twang and cadences to perfection. She told a good story. Many of the unnamed sources for Coolidge anecdotes were via Grace. A good sense of humor, either as the teller or tellee, stands everyone, First Lady or not, in good stead. It relieves strain, puts people at ease, and keeps things in proper perspective. Grace was pretty good at it.

Being governor of Massachusetts had been the pinnacle of Coolidge's ambition, but during a police strike at the end of World War I, he announced that "there is no right to strike against the public safety by anybody, anywhere, any time."

That one statement catapulted him into national prominence. He was seriously touted as presidential material. Grace, as usual, was still in the dark. When he told her he was being nominated as the Republican vice presidential candidate in 1920, she was stunned. "But you aren't going to accept, are you?" she asked. He replied, "I think I have to."

No two people enjoyed the vice presidency more than the Coolidges. They were content with living in a Washington hotel suite. Presiding over the Senate was easy, particularly for a man who weathered boredom well. The rest of the job was devoted to ceremony: ribbon cutting, ground breaking, hand-shaking, and dining out. "Gotta eat somewhere," the frugal Coolidge said, and they accepted all invitations that came their way. With Grace's good looks and appealing personality coupled with the agonizingly dry wit that would make Silent Cal legendary, the Second Family were immensely popular. They were everybody's guests of honor, and since they were not required to return invitations very often, it kept their grocery budget to a minimum.

When Coolidge became president after the sudden death of Warren Harding, it coincided with two important events. First, Coolidge was the first president to benefit from a separate budget for entertaining. Previous presidents had to pay those expenses out of their own pocket. Second, the Roaring Twenties were in full swing, flooding the country with a spate of pop culture. With the inundation of movies, radio, vaudeville, sports teams, and flagpole sitters came an army of famous personalities—all of whom wanted to shake hands and be photographed with the president. It was a curious juxtaposition, since Calvin and Grace were the antithesis of that era. They neither roared nor flapped. But the celebrities came in droves. Calvin was happy to shake hands, accept their token gifts, and take a photo wearing a sombrero or Indian headdress, believing it humanized him. Grace was happy to invite them to stay to lunch or dinner. It was she who kept the conversation going at the table. She read their books and magazine stories, saw their movies and shows, listened to their radio programs, and checked the scorecards. She would ask pertinent questions and make suitable comments. Knowing her husband's communication skills were nil, it would be her sole responsibility to make the White House table talk appealing. This she did time and again, and for that she was widely admired and well liked. So, for that matter, was he.

"Don't try anything new, Grace," Coolidge had said at the start of his presidency, so she didn't. She made no speeches nor held any press conferences. She was forbidden to wear trousers or smoke cigarettes. She was content to host tea parties and ladies' luncheons and do whatever Calvin told her to do. When she had the temerity to ask for a copy of his daily schedule, he was shocked. "We don't give that information out indiscriminately, Grace," he said. It never occurred to him that it might be disrespectful to his wife, but she never seemed to consider his attitude demeaning. She kept her hat and purse handy in order to be ready at a moment's notice whenever she was needed. And he took her everywhere. Her photograph, usually holding a ubiquitous bouquet, was seen everywhere. Only in her midforties, she presented a good-looking image for the newsreels.

But popular or not, once retired from the White House, Grace was promptly forgotten. She would outlive her husband by a quarter century, and now she tried new things. She wrote some magazine articles of her own. During World War II she volunteered with the Red Cross and raised funds for refugee children. She flew in a plane and went to Europe. She became an active trustee for the School for the Deaf where she had once taught. She even kissed a Democrat. A youthful Jack Kennedy campaigned in her area, and the peck on the cheek made headlines.

Postscript: HOWARD CHANDLER CHRISTY PAINTED GRACE'S OFFICIAL PORTRAIT WITH AN UNCHARACTER- ISTIC SERIOUS EXPRESSION. WHEN ASKED ABOUT IT, HE COMMENTED, "I THOUGHT I ONCE SAW A LOOK OF RESIGNATION ON HER FACE."

LOU HOOVER
1874–1944

FIRST LADY: 1929–33

The Unsung Hero

With only daughters in pioneer California of the 1880s, Charles Henry taught Lou, his tall, athletic oldest daughter, to camp, fish, ride, shoot, and build a fire. Since he was a well-to-do banker, he also provided her with the finer things, including a normal school education so the bright girl could become a teacher.

After only a year of teaching, Lou chanced to attend a lecture on geology and was entranced. She persuaded her family to enroll her at Stanford University, where she met Herbert Hoover and changed her life's direction. They were the same age, but he was a senior, she a freshman. Their attraction was immediate but more friendly than romantic, since the pathetically shy Bert was poor and had no money to conduct a proper courtship. Somehow Lou instinctively knew he was a man with promise and determined to "major in Herbert Hoover." When he graduated, he embarked on a series of demanding mining engineering jobs in exotic lands, and they agreed to correspond. By the time Lou graduated, Bert was no longer poor, nor would he ever be again. Now earning $40,000 a year, he was well able to support a wife. It was 1899; they were both twenty-five.

Their honeymoon took them to China, and for the next two decades, apart from brief visits home, they lived abroad, often in remote locations. As a degreed geologist herself, Lou helped her mining engineer husband compile his reports and catalog his samples. She also studied the culture of each of the lands where they lived. The Hoovers circumnavigated the globe twice. To pass the time on less-than-luxury liners, they translated a rare Renaissance mining treatise from its original Latin. In addition to being intelligent, curious, and rugged, Lou was also an excellent linguist. She became fluent in six languages, including two Chinese dialects. Their translated book would be a bestseller—in mining circles.

By 1914 Hoover owned his own mining consultancy, with offices in six countries. At forty, he was a millionaire several times over and living in London's posh Mayfair district. Lou had carved out a place for herself, raising two sons, managing a household awash in servants, entertaining nearly every night, and volunteering her time and services for various charitable causes. The beginning of World War I in Europe, however, altered their lives permanently. With more than one hundred thousand Americans stranded on the warring continent, London became the last stop and swarmed with Yanks desperate to get home. British officials recruited Hoover to help his fellow countrymen, and he immediately agreed. He had found his true calling, and Lou would find hers: humanitarianism on a massive scale. Herbert Hoover would never again work as a mining engineer, and Lou's activities would forevermore have a larger purpose in mind.

Both of them were blessed with high energy, good health, and extraordinary administrative talents. Independent wealth gave them latitude. While Bert assumed responsibilities for helping Americans return to the States, Lou undertook the task of alleviating their short-term needs. Soliciting help from dozens of well-to-do London women, she set up day nurseries at railroad stations, arranged for food, coffee, milk, and diapers, and made sure everything ran smoothly. She would be the only woman to have a seat on the executive board established for the overall repatriation project.

Once the American emergency ended, the Hoovers faced an even larger crisis. The German army had overrun tiny Belgium, laying waste to everything and leaving its starving population homeless, fuel-less, helpless, and hopeless. Now the Hoovers would undertake the gargantuan task of rescuing that beleaguered country. While Bert focused on arranging shiploads of humanitarian supplies and all the diplomatic finagling to permit those ships to pass unmolested by the German U-boats, Lou shuttled back and forth to America, making speeches to raise money, food, and clothing.

Lou's Legacy

Lou Hoover is arguably the least known of the twentieth-century First Ladies despite a long list of serious and consequential achievements. It is said that both Hoovers were the victims of their innately shy personalities. Lou's sense of propriety and **MODESTY** precluded any possibility of tooting her own horn, or even allowing someone else to toot it for her. The light of her intelligence, generosity, executive skills, and activism was always hidden under the proverbial bushel. Modesty aside, she deserves better.

By the time America entered the war in 1917, Herbert Hoover was already famous. After his success in helping feed Belgium, President Wilson summoned him home to help make the United States the world's breadbasket. Lou, now a practiced speaker, would also be a contributor to countless publications about how the war effort could be helped on the home front. When the urgencies abated by 1919, she turned her energies elsewhere.

Lou Hoover had been familiar with the Girl Guides during

her years in London. Once home, she decided her own out-door upbringing was a natural fit for the recently formed American Girl Scouts. She volunteered as a scout leader but rose quickly in their executive ranks. She worked long and hard, helping to plan policies and programs, and using her established notoriety to generate publicity for the scouts. In short order she became its national president, and under her leadership, membership increased more than tenfold.

Between Bert's cabinet office during the Harding and Coolidge Administrations and her civic leadership through-out the 1920s, both Hoovers had become household words when he was elected president in 1928. No two people had higher expectations heaped on their shoulders. Where Calvin Coolidge had one secretary, Hoover brought three. Grace Coolidge needed no secretary, but Lou brought two, and one more would be added—all paid by the Hoovers person-ally. (Neither of them ever accepted compensation for their humanitarian or governmental positions.)

When the dam of prosperity broke, the floodwaters of the Great Depression came in biblical proportions. The remarkable reputations of both Bert and Lou Hoover became mired in its sludge. Progressive in outlook but conserva-tive in personality, magnanimous in practice but reticent by nature, neither of them were equipped to provide the dynamic leadership necessary for this crisis. Nor were they inclined to challenge years of accepted first family behavior, particularly *Republican* first family behavior. They would absorb the abuse, and if and when they fought back, theirs would be a weak, weaponless fight. They could never have behaved otherwise.

As the Depression deepened, Lou began receiving hundreds of letters begging for her help. "Help my husband get a job." "Help my children get shoes." "The roof needs repair." "We need warm coats." "We have no food." The list seemed endless. A third secretary was quietly engaged to help Lou review and respond to all the pressing needs. Many were referred, with Lou's card, to government agencies, various charities, women's clubs, and of course the Girl Scouts. Hundreds of requests were met with Lou's personal check for a few dollars or packages of shoes and clothing or vouchers for food and fuel. When it was suggested that she make this effort public, both Hoovers were horrified at the notion of promoting their private generosity.

The huge and unselfish contributions both Hoovers made to the country have long been unrecognized, eclipsed by the vibrant Franklin and Eleanor Roosevelt and their New Deal. It is only today, seventy-five years later, that historians have begun to realize the raw deal that befell such fine people.

Postscript: LOU HOOVER DIED SUDDENLY, SHORTLY BEFORE HER SEVENTIETH BIRTHDAY. WHEN HER HUS-BAND SORTED THROUGH HER DESK, HE DISCOVERED HUNDREDS OF CHECKS FOR SMALL AMOUNTS SENT BY PRIVATE INDIVIDUALS TO REPAY HER FAVORS, KINDNESSES, AND SUPPORT. SOME HAD BEEN LYING AROUND FOR YEARS. LOU HAD NEVER CASHED THEM.

ELEANOR ROOSEVELT
1884–1962

FIRST LADY: 1933–45

The Incomparable Mrs. R.

It is interesting to wonder how different the world might
be had Eleanor Roosevelt looked like her mother. Young,
beautiful, flamboyant New York socialite Anna Hall married
Theodore Roosevelt's younger brother, Elliott, but it would be
a tragic union. Elliott was addicted to alcohol and laudanum.
While he dearly loved his plain and very serious-looking
daughter, who he called "little Nell," he needed to live apart
from the family. It would be a loveless and Dickensian childhood for the little girl. Anna Hall died when Eleanor was six.
Her addicted father would die when she was ten, leaving her

to be raised by her somewhat dotty Grandmother Hall and some equally dotty Hall aunts and uncles. Well-meaning hospitality from the rambunctious Roosevelt side made the timid child uncomfortable, and Eleanor seemed cocooned in an internal world, growing too tall, too gangly, and too plain, with a hopeless overbite.

Nevertheless she was sent to a good finishing school in England, where she was an excellent student. To her surprise, the withdrawn young girl became popular with her classmates. These were the happiest three years of her youth. After being "finished," Eleanor returned home to reluctantly make her obligatory debut into the fashionable society where she was temperamentally unsuited. Since her upbringing precluded actual employment, she joined the Junior League, whose activities were charitable and thus acceptable. She volunteered at the settlement houses on New York's Lower East Side that teemed with old tenements and new immigrants and found her calling: being useful. She began making daily trips downtown.

A chance meeting with her fifth cousin Franklin Delano Roosevelt blossomed into romance, despite strong opposition from Franklin's domineering mother. In Sara Delano's eyes, no one was good enough for her son, especially someone as homely, unstylish, socially inept, and financially underwhelming as Eleanor. They married anyway, when Eleanor was twenty. She bore six children within ten years.

Overpowered by her intimidating mother-in-law, Eleanor lived in the shadows. Granny ran the house and children. It would not be until she was nearly forty, and her husband had been stricken by polio, that Eleanor emerged to become *Eleanor*. Despite a marriage that had evolved into a pattern of separate lives, both Roosevelts maintained an exceptional working relationship and a genuine friendship. She discovered political talents she never knew she had. Combined with her innate intelligence and desire to help alleviate human suffering, she had developed into a powerful force in her own right more than a decade before she became First Lady. She would become her husband's eyes and ears, a task she understood, relished, and made her own.

Still, some things needed to be learned. If she were to be his eyes and ears, she would need to develop a sense of smell as well—that intangible sense of learning by experience. One story tells that shortly after FDR became Democratic governor of New York in 1929, he sent Eleanor to visit the prisons that came under his jurisdiction. She returned laden with charts and reports, but the governor wanted to hear her impressions—not look at paperwork. "Did you inspect the kitchens?" he asked. She said yes. "How was the food?" "Very good," she replied and produced several weeks of menus. "Did you look in the pot, Eleanor? Did you taste it?" She hadn't and thus learned what she considered a valuable lesson: anyone can write beef stew on a piece of paper; it does not mean they prepared it properly. Eleanor would develop a remarkable ability to smell it; to grasp the essence of a situation, learn from it, and apply that lesson elsewhere. She would also have seemingly endless opportunities to put those lessons into practice.

The list of her accomplishments and activities could and have filled volumes.

Eleanor's Legacy

Eleanor Roosevelt is of course a benchmark for all First Ladies. The list of her achievements is a long one that may never be surpassed. But of all her considerable attributes, the only one that is hers alone among the "old" First Ladies is **A VERY THICK HIDE**. Mary Lincoln dissolved in tears, and Edith Wilson openly groused at criticism, but Eleanor was born for her role. No other First Lady was so harshly, consistently, and publicly reviled and ridiculed for her failure to behave according to traditional womanly standards. But none were as capable as Eleanor of withstanding the attacks with equanimity and moving ahead, doing whatever she had in mind anyway, without allowing it to upset her emotionally or interfere with her overall purpose. It is no small consideration.

When FDR became president in 1933, the Depression was crippling the country. Thousands of Depression-burdened veterans from the Great War had descended on Washington. They set up shanty camps and demanded immediate payment of their promised bonuses. The problem was that the bonuses were not due for another decade. The Hoover administration had sent the army to disperse them, but Roosevelt had sent "His Missus." Eleanor showed up with coffee and sandwiches and sympathy.

Mrs. R. never inspired neutrality. For the millions who adored her, there were thousands of her countrymen and women who believed she was not only a traitor to her class but to women in general. Other First Ladies had behaved properly, knowing their place was in the respectable background. Eleanor was visible. She traveled constantly to rural areas, mines, sharecropping towns—wherever poverty had left its mark and help was needed. Once the United States entered World War II, she even traveled to the war zones. The military brass was adamantly opposed to her presence in the field hospitals, but they soon became her most ardent supporters. She was useful. The soldiers loved her. She faithfully wrote personal letters to the families of every soldier she met. There were hundreds. Not only did she go everywhere and do everything, she wrote a daily newspaper column about it. She gave press conferences with generous regularity. She had grown comfortable in the public spotlight and knew how to use it.

Wherever she went, Eleanor regularly purchased small objects from local craftsmen. The five- and ten-cent items were always laid aside as token gifts for White House staff members and their families. No one was ever neglected by Mrs. Roosevelt. Despite all her activities, despite the demands on her time, despite the usual carping from the usual complainers, Eleanor never forgot a family birthday or anniversary or crisis. Mother R. remembered every grandchild and every godchild. Gifts were sent. Calls were made. Bedsides were visited. She even remembered every in-law. Her five grown children would have eighteen marriages among them, not a sterling comment on marital felicity. Perhaps learning from her own chilly relationship with Sara Delano, Eleanor was nonjudgmental, cordial, and welcoming. Even the "exes" had kind words for their mother-in-law.

Widowed in her early sixties, Eleanor continued her exhausting schedule, but now on a worldwide level. President Truman appointed her as a delegate to the newly created United Nations. She promoted whatever worthwhile cause came her way and went looking for any that might have been overlooked. She was definitely useful.

Postscript: ELEANOR WAS ASKED ONCE TO COMMENT ON THE MOST IMPORTANT ATTRIBUTE A FIRST LADY NEEDS. NEVER GIVEN TO PLATITUDES OR BANALITIES, SHE SURPRISED THE INTERVIEWER BY QUICKLY SAYING, "GOOD HEALTH." THE DEMANDS OF BEING THE FIRST LADY ARE SO GREAT THAT SHE DOESN'T HAVE TIME TO BE SICK. TOO MANY PEOPLE ARE DEPENDING ON HER.

BESS TRUMAN
1885–1982

FIRST LADY: 1945–53

Reluctant Lady

Bess Truman was a throwback to a past century. She was less than comfortable in her position as society leader, and she positively loathed the intrusive fishbowl life of the White House. She had a secret to protect.

When Bess Wallace was eighteen, her alcoholic father committed suicide. It was a huge scandal in Independence, Missouri, at the turn of the twentieth century, particularly since her mother was a Gates, one of the wealthiest and most prominent midwestern families. Madge Wallace was a difficult, demanding, and generally peculiar woman on her best day, and after that horrible episode, she would become worse. Bess was needed at home. It would fall to her to manage the household, which included her three younger brothers. Whatever future plans she may have had fell by the wayside. They moved into the stately Gates Mansion with her elderly grandparents.

Bess had known Harry Truman since early childhood. They were classmates, but Harry was just a poor farm boy, so their social contact was superficial. He was far beneath the posh and generally snobbish Wallace family. It wasn't until both were in their midtwenties that he began courting her. It would be a very long courtship, since Harry had his own family obligations and still had no money. In addition, Mrs. Wallace was less than enthusiastic about her daughter keeping company with a farmer from the wrong side of the tracks.

It would not be until after World War I when both were in their midthirties that they would finally marry—and then they would live with Mrs. Wallace in the old Gates Mansion. Bess refused to leave her eccentric mother by herself, and no one else could live with her. Harry reluctantly agreed and never uttered a disparaging word, not even when the old lady insisted on sitting at the head of the dining room table.

Despite having "the original mother-in-law from hell," according to Truman's friends, Harry and Bess had a happy and companionable marriage. They were comfortable with each other. She did girl-things, he did guy-things. Bess was content in her small world, which included a group of childhood friends who were accustomed to Madge Wallace and came to play bridge regularly. Harry made a niche for himself as a local political administrator and found a bunch of political pals who met once or twice a week at the local hotel to play nickel poker and sip whiskey. He was never drunk, nor did he lose much money. Bess was glad to have him get out and enjoy himself. But there would never be any dinner guests invited to what was now called the Wallace Mansion.

When Harry was elected to the U.S. Senate in the 1930s, he went alone. Bess was still reluctant to leave her mother. She finally made a visit to Washington and was surprisingly delighted, so Harry rented a larger apartment during the next session, and the Trumans and their teenaged daughter, Margaret, came to the capital. So did Mrs. Wallace. But in *their* apartment, Harry could sit at the head of his own table.

Always preferring to remain in the background, Bess nevertheless made friends among the congressional wives, especially when they discovered what a crackerjack bridge player she was. She also began helping out in Harry's Senate office, handling his personal correspondence and guiding visiting Missourians around town. Still, Bess and her mother made frequent trips back to Independence. It was home. It was where she belonged.

In April 1945, FDR died suddenly, and the Truman lives were abruptly altered. Harry had been the surprise nominee for vice president during the 1944 election, and now, barely three months later, he was president. Bess was sixty, and she was not about to change. Much was expected of her, especially after the overwhelming presence of her predecessor, who kindly offered to help the new First Lady through her first press conference.

It would be her first and last. Bess requested all questions be submitted in writing, and with the exception of listing her wedding date, everything was answered with "No comment." She was monosyllabic and guarded. She believed the questions were either impertinent or nobody's business and said so. She dreaded the thought that her father's suicide some forty-odd years earlier would be dredged up by nosy reporters and cause her mother anguish all over again. The elderly woman had come to live with them in the White House, still completely unimpressed with farmer Truman, who she never called Harry and who was still totally unacceptable in her eyes.

Bess let it be known (at least to Harry) that she would be happy to undertake whatever tasks were assigned to her in the way of formal dinners and receptions, teas and receiving lines, managing the household, and the usual ribbon cutting and bouquet receiving. But that would be it. She declared that her biggest responsibility was seeing that her hat was on straight. With the crushing duties befalling Truman and keeping him perpetually occupied, their solid companionship suffered. His days seemed endless, and whether his aides planned it consciously or not, a wedge was driven between the close couple. The president had little time for his wife, so Bess and her mother escaped to Independence as often as they could. She was, by her own admission, a homebody who preferred the security of her limited surroundings and tight circle of old friends. Their daughter Margaret, now past twenty, was thrilled to fill in at social obligations in lieu of her absent mother.

Bess's Legacy

It might be curious, given the example of Abigail Adams or Eleanor Roosevelt, to credit Bess Truman of all people with **INDEPENDENCE**, but she was undeniably an independent person. Small-world homebody that she was, she cared nothing about anybody's opinion except Harry's, and periodically even that was up for discussion. Things would usually go her way. Like Jacqueline Kennedy a decade later, she would escape the White House for weeks at a time. On the campaign trail, Harry used to introduce her as "The Boss," a reference she hated. He did it anyway. He was pretty independent too.

The only lasting impression history retains of Bess Truman is the newsreel image of a stout, sixty-something woman, christening a new C-54 airplane, whacking away with a champagne bottle that refused to break. Initially outraged and embarrassed, she complained to the president, who immediately demanded a copy of the film. He would not have his wife, the First Lady of the land, humiliated. When Harry, Bess, and Margaret viewed the footage, tears rolled down their faces as they convulsed with laughter. No one was laughing at Bess; they were laughing at a hysterically funny situation. It is still funny. First Ladies have done far worse than giving the country a good belly laugh.

The Trumans spent most of Harry's second term living in the Blair House across the street from the White House. Fifty years after Theodore Roosevelt's renovations, the old mansion again needed extensive structural repair. Bess took little if any part in the planning or details. It was not her house. She was not interested. Harry was the one who loved making frequent inspection tours of the renovations. It was arguably the one part of his turbulent presidency that he truly enjoyed. Bess would do her duty and whatever Harry asked of her, no less but not one bit more. She was poor copy for the media, and they grew tired of her. Most of her photographs show her with a generally sullen expression. When Truman's term in office ended, she breathed a huge sigh of relief. She could go home and would never leave again. When she died, she was nearly a hundred. Our longest-lived First Lady.

Postscript: OLD LADY WALLACE DIED ONLY WEEKS BEFORE THE INAUGURATION OF A NEW PRESIDENT IN 1953. SHE WAS PAST NINETY. SHE LEFT HER HOUSE TO BESS. NOW IT WOULD OFFICIALLY BE THE TRUMAN MANSION. AND IT REALLY ISN'T A MANSION. IT'S JUST A NICE OLD HOUSE.

MAMIE EISENHOWER
1896–1979

FIRST LADY: 1953–61

The Grandma Next Door

Mamie Doud was one of those spoiled little rich girls. She grew up in the most fashionable section of Denver, Colorado, one of four daughters. A childhood bout of rheumatic fever left her vigilant about her health, and she would always be inclined to pamper herself and take to her bed at the slightest sniffle.

She was barely eighteen when she met Lt. Dwight Eisenhower, recently graduated from West Point, but the attraction was immediate and powerful. They married a year later. The Douds adored the handsome officer, but they had concerns about Mamie's ability, or inability, to adapt to the hardships of army life. It would not be an easy adjustment. The Eisenhowers would move twenty times in twenty years and wouldn't even own a house until shortly before Ike became president—when he was past sixty! While housekeeping would never be high on Mamie's list of preferences or talents, once Ike rose high enough in the ranks to have domestic help, she surprised herself on what a fine supervisor she could become.

The life of a junior officer, and a farm boy at that, is far from affluent, and Mamie had to learn early on how to tighten their belts and make do, grateful for an occasional check from home. She developed a legendary thrift (some called it stingy), shopped sales, clipped coupons, and was proud to announce that she bought her dresses off the rack. With a small house to manage and time on her hands, Mamie fell in with a group of officers' wives for card parties and luncheons. Ike and Mamie were definitely sociable, and they fit in easily wherever they were deployed. They entertained so often that their home (wherever it was) was nicknamed Club Eisenhower.

Between the two World Wars, military promotions were like molasses. During the Depression, no soldier in his right mind would voluntarily give up such a steady income, no matter how small, especially since there were no wars to be fought. Ike would be a major for a long time, and he reconciled himself to the fact that he would probably retire no higher than a colonel. Still he always managed to come to the attention of his superiors, who invariably recommended him for special training or assignments. Ike did not disappoint. They kept an eye on him. Mamie was perfectly happy just being Mrs. Ike.

Mamie's Legacy

Given the example of Eleanor Roosevelt before her and the fifty years of substantive First Ladies who followed, Mamie Eisenhower's few accomplishments crumble in the dust. She was the figure of a First Lady in transition, and perhaps the only one who was so well suited to it. She was the first First Lady who presented an **IMAGE**—something no previous First Lady needed to have. Her bangs and her sweet smile and petite figure were a far cry from the generally unattractive-looking First Ladies who had preceded her for a generation. She was the epitome of a brief and happy time, when Ike and Mamie were in the White House and all seemed well with the world.

Once the Second World War began and stars attached themselves to Ike's shoulders, Mamie's biggest challenge was coping with five years of separation, anxiety, and loneliness. Ike was stationed overseas, and Mamie never knew if or when he might be in harm's way, particularly since cities were targets rather than battlefields, and Ike had discovered the joys of flying. Always inclined to be a worrier, Mamie was constantly on edge. She lost more than twenty pounds, which made her petite frame look emaciated. She also had to duck the invariable reporters who were eager for information (which she never had), color stories about the great general (which she never gave), or her opinions on different situations (which she seldom had and never offered). She led a secluded life, playing interminable games of canasta and mah-jongg and pooling ration cards with other officers' wives for their regular hen parties. Then the rumors started. First came talk that Ike was romantically involved with his pretty driver. Then it was reported that Mrs. Ike had a drinking problem. All evidence points to the contrary in both cases, and they both chose to ignore the gossip as beneath their dignity. But Americans have an insatiable lust for dirt about their icons, so the rumors persist even today.

By the end of the War, Ike had five stars and was a leading political candidate, an offer he steadfastly refused to consider for more than five years. For the first time in their lives, they were financially comfortable, thanks in part to the huge success of Ike's wartime memoirs, *Crusade in Europe*. They bought a farm in Gettysburg, Pennsylvania, which they loved fixing up. They were also middle-aged grandparents. But what a picture they presented! They were *America's* grandparents. Mamie in her midfifties was cute as a button, even glamorous, with her trademark bangs that became all the rage. She didn't need to buy off the rack anymore, but she still did occasionally. Whatever she wore looked good on her and was copied. She loved pink, and pink became the in-color of the 1950s.

Finally Ike relented and announced his candidacy. Surprising everyone, including herself, Mamie proved to be a great campaigner. She seldom complained of being tired. She loved waving to the crowds, grinning ear to ear—just like Ike. After all those years of wartime separation, she was thrilled to be at her husband's side, and she was not about to let any aides push her into the background. Nor was she about to be separated from her husband for any length of time again. Politicians quickly realized what an asset she was by "just being Mamie." The crowds ate it up and everybody loved her.

Ike was elected to the presidency twice—both times by huge landslides. All the great people of the world came to call at the White House, but by now most of them were longtime personal friends. It was like Club Eisenhower again, only more formal, located at a better address. Ike the President and Mamie the First Lady were exactly what the country wanted and needed in the nervous postwar 1950s: a return to whatever they may have thought was normal and, for certain, a leap of faith into the hope of a better world. Mamie was adorable, the antithesis of grande dame Lou Hoover, do-gooder Eleanor Roosevelt, and scowling Bess Truman. Mamie still had a waistline. It did not matter if she never wore an apron or baked cookies. She looked like someone who did and would. If Ike the Hero had become the grandpa-patriarch of the American family, then Mamie was obviously the grandma.

But other than her family, which she dearly loved, it would

be their one and only house in Gettysburg that filled Mamie's heart. All the furniture that had been collected bit by bit over forty years could finally and permanently come out of storage. All their collections and gifts accumulated from worldwide travel could find a home. They could be Ma and Pa Kettle and entertain the people they truly liked without needing to play the role. Since they liked practically everybody, it wasn't hard. They could even play cards or watch television on their sunporch, eating TV dinners on snack trays. They were as American as apple pie and would be forever beloved.

They did not know it then, but an era was passing. Presidents and First Ladies would no longer command regard and respect in the same way. Television, jet travel, modern conveniences, and instant communication would speed up life itself, trading true leadership for the sound bites of what makes media headlines. Mamie brought no special achievements to be recorded in the annals of American life. She was just the epitome of America itself.

Postscript: MAMIE EISENHOWER TOOK IKE "IN SICK-NESS AND IN HEALTH" WHEN THEY MARRIED. SHE OBVI-OUSLY MEANT IT. IKE HAD A HEART ATTACK WHEN HE WAS PRESIDENT, AND AS HE DETERIORATED THROUGH THE YEARS, IF IKE WAS IN THE HOSPITAL, MAMIE MOVED INTO AN ADJOINING ROOM. NO MORE SEPARA-TIONS. SHE EVEN BROUGHT HER PINK BED JACKET.

AUTHOR'S NOTE

Writing a brief volume about some of the lesser known First Ladies presents a challenge on several fronts. Some explanation to the reader is in order.

First: Economy. This book is not intended to be a litany of almanac facts. All the pertinent details of birth, death, marriage, and related information are readily available about these women elsewhere. The challenge is thus twofold: a) to make each of these fine (and usually neglected) women come to life in a thousand words or so, and b) to avoid the redundancies of their lives in general. Faced with few opportunities to command attention on their own, their lives became similar to each other and to their contemporaries. They grew up, married, bore and raised children, and suffered the usual slings and arrows.

In order to keep the reader interested, huge and important historic events may be glossed over in a brief phrase, e.g., "after the Civil War." Sometimes including certain important episodes tends to lead down a channel from which it can be difficult to extricate oneself in a brief sentence or two. Sometimes it is just more feasible to avoid them entirely. Many excellent sources provide in-depth consideration.

The whole idea then is to focus on that part of each First Lady's personality or life segment or accomplishment or whatever made her unique among her sister Ladies. It is truly a challenge to surgically cut without killing the patient.

Second: Why end with Mamie Eisenhower? This is a personal choice. I decided long ago to limit my scholarship with the Eisenhowers. They were the last presidential couple born in the nineteenth century, which makes it as good a place as any to put a period at the end of a sentence.

More importantly, it becomes increasingly obvious as time goes on that Ike and Mamie were the end of an era. With the 1960s came an explosion of instant communication, television, transportation, and an all-consuming in-your-face media. The rules changed. The expectations changed. The role of a pleasant-looking housewife who could be a graceful hostess or accepter of bouquets became irrelevant. Now a First Lady had to be attractive. If she wasn't blessed with the face and figure of Jacqueline Kennedy, she would have handlers assigned to oversee her diet, her complexion, her hair and wardrobe, and make her an "image." She was expected to be educated, politically savvy and well-schooled in high-level diplomacy. She was expected to lend her name, her time, and her prestige to some noncontroversial social or cultural or civic issues on her own, such as ecology or education. And finally, she was expected to be everywhere, doing everything, every day, dressed and coiffed to perfection, with a smile on her face. The eyes of the world were upon her. She could no longer be a private person, and she had better measure up. She could never get sick, tired, irritable, angry, sad, or, heaven forbid, bored. No more free rides for a First Lady. These new "qualifications" are not about to change.

Furthermore, many of the post-Mamie First Ladies have written their own books, and dozens have been written about them. Some are praising; some are downright vicious. No aspect of their lives is off-limits to prying eyes. Truth does not even have to be in the mix. We probably know more than enough about every detail, and I, personally, do not wish to dredge for sludge. Our First Ladies are entitled to whatever shreds of privacy remain to them.

Therefore, more than a century of very nice "old gals" have been summarily rejected as non-entities, a disparaging and often untrue connotation. Some excellent scholars have begun to research deeply into the contributions of some of those neglected presidential wives, in an effort to revitalize the perceived role of women in an age when they were vital only to propagate the race and make men more comfortable. In other words, an age when women were mothers first, then adornments worn on the arm of their prosperous husbands. *The First Ladies*, with its condensed chapters, is not meant to be compared to these academic achievements. This is not a dissertation. It is an hors d'oeuvre.

Finally: Their "legacies." These are not legacies of tangible accomplishment. How can any one of the early First Ladies compete with the seemingly endless list of Eleanor Roosevelt's substantial activities? Pitting these "old gals" against our modern First Ladies only serves to trivialize them and make them seem even more inconsequential.

They were definitely *not* inconsequential. They were paragons for their times and must be considered in that context. They were what every man wanted his wife to be like, what every parent wanted their daughters to be like, and what every little girl wanted to be like when she grew up. That, in itself, is *very* consequential.

The "legacies," therefore, are those of character or personality that are worthy of emulation. They are not mere banalities. Some may be qualities that many of them share, but I have tried to assign them to that particular Lady who best personified the trait. Every one of our old First Ladies had something to offer, if only to her husband. In many cases, an audience of one was enough.

And finally, my overwhelming aim in *The First Ladies* is to make these mini-lives of our old First Ladies readable, readable, and then readable. If someone is inspired to read further, dig deeper, or want to know more, I have accomplished my purpose.

-FSF

BIBLIOGRAPHY

Allgor, Catherine. *Parlor Politics: In Which the Ladies of Washington Help Build a City and a Government.* Charlottesville: University of Virginia Press, 2000.

———. *A Perfect Union.* New York: Henry Holt & Co., 2006.

Anthony, Carl Sferrazza. *First Ladies: The Saga of the Presidents' Wives and Their Power, 1789–1961.* New York: Morrow, 1990.

———. *Florence Harding: The First Lady, the Jazz Age, and the Death of America's Most Scandalous President.* New York: Morrow, 1998.

———. *Nellie Taft: The Unconventional First Lady of the Ragtime Era.* New York: Morrow, 2005.

Anthony, Katharine. *Dolley Madison.* Garden City, NY: Doubleday, 1949.

Barzman, Sol. *The First Ladies.* New York: Cowles, 1970.

Bobbe, Dorothie. *Mr. and Mrs. John Quincy Adams: An Adventure in Patriotism.* New York: Minton, Balch & Co., 1950.

Boller, Paul F., Jr. *Presidential Campaigns.* New York: Oxford University Press, 1985.

———. *Presidential Wives: An Anecdotal History.* New York: Oxford University Press, 1988.

Bourne, Miriam Anne. *First Family: George Washington and His Intimate Relations.* New York: Norton, 1982.

Brady, Patricia. *Martha Washington: An American Life.* New York: Viking Press, 2005.

Brandon, Dorothy. *Mamie Doud Eisenhower: A Portrait of a First Lady.* New York: Scribner, 1954.

Brands, H. W. *Andrew Jackson: His Life and Times.* New York: Doubleday, 2005.

———. *TR: The Last Romantic.* New York: Basic Books, 1997.

Britton, Nan. *The President's Daughter.* New York: Guild, 1927.

Brodsky, Alyn. *Grover Cleveland: A Study in Character.* New York: St. Martin's Press, 2000.

Brown, Rita Mae. *Dolley: A Novel of Dolley Madison in Love and War.* New York: Bantam, 1994.

Bunting, Josiah, III. *Ulysses S. Grant.* New York: Times Books, 2004.

Butt, Archibald W. *Taft and Roosevelt: The Intimate Letters of Archie Butt, Military Aide.* 2 vols. Garden City, NY: Doubleday, Doran & Co., 1930.

Butterfield, L. H., Marc Friedlaender, and Mary-Jo Kline, eds. *The Book of Abigail and John: Selected Letters of the Adams*

Family, 1762–1784. Cambridge, MA: Harvard University Press, 1975.

Byrd, Max. *Grant: A Novel*. New York: Bantam Books, 2000.

———. *Jackson: A Novel*. New York: Bantam Books, 2002.

Caroli, Betty Boyd. *America's First Ladies*. Garden City, NY: Doubleday, 1996.

———. *First Ladies*. New York: Oxford University Press, 1995.

———. *Inside the White House: America's Most Famous Home, the First 200 Years*. Garden City, NY: Doubleday, 1994.

———. *The Roosevelt Women*. New York: Basic Books, 1998.

Carpenter, Frank G. *Carp's Washington*. New York: McGraw-Hill, 1960.

Chadwick, Bruce. *The General and Mrs. Washington: The Untold Story of a Marriage and a Revolution*. Naperville, IL: Sourcebooks, 2007.

Clinton, Catherine. *Mrs. Lincoln: A Life*. New York: Harper, 2009.

Colver, Anne. *Mr. Lincoln's Wife*. 1943. Reprint, New York: Holt, Rinehart and Winston, 1965.

Conwell, Russell H. *Life and Public Services of Governor Rutherford B. Hayes*. Boston: B. B. Russell, 1876.

Daugherty, Harry. *The Inside Story of the Harding Tragedy*. New York: Churchill Company, 1932.

David, Lester, and Irene David. *Ike and Mamie: The Story of the General and His Lady.* New York: Putnam, 1981.

Davis, Burke. *Old Hickory: A Life of Andrew Jackson.* New York: Dial Press, 1977.

Desmond, Alice Curtis. *Glamorous Dolley Madison.* New York: Dodd, Mead, 1965.

Donald, David. *Lincoln.* New York: Simon & Schuster, 1995.

Eisenhower, Dwight D. *Letters to Mamie.* Garden City, NY: Doubleday, 1978.

Eisenhower, Susan. *Mrs. Ike: Memories and Reflections on the Life of Mamie Eisenhower.* New York: Farrar, Straus and Giroux, 1996.

Ellis, Joseph. *Passionate Sage: The Character and Legacy of John Adams.* New York: Norton, 1993.

Emerson, Edwin. *Hoover and His Times: Looking Back through the Years.* Garden City, NY: Garden City Publishing, 1932.

Epstein, Daniel Mark. *The Lincolns: Portrait of a Marriage.* New York: Ballantine Books, 2008.

Falkner, Leonard. *The President Who Wouldn't Retire: John Quincy Adams: Congressman from Massachusetts.* New York: Coward-McCann, 1967.

Freud, Sigmund, and William C. Bullitt. *Thomas Woodrow Wilson: A Psychological Study.* Boston: Houghton Mifflin, 1967.

Fuess, Claude M. *Calvin Coolidge: The Man from Vermont.* Boston: Little, Brown & Co., 1940.

Furman, Bess. *White House Profile: A Social History of the United States, Its Occupants and Its Festivities.* Indianapolis: Bobbs-Merrill, 1951.

Garrison, Webb. *White House Ladies: Fascinating Tales and Colorful Curiosities.* Nashville: Rutledge Hill Press, 1996.

Geer, Emily Apt. *First Lady: The Life of Lucy Webb Hayes.* Kent, OH: Kent State University Press, 1984.

Gerson, Noel B. *The Velvet Glove.* Nashville: Thomas Nelson, 1975.

Goldhurst, Richard. *Many Are the Hearts: The Agony and the Triumph of Ulysses S. Grant.* New York: Readers Digest Press, 1975.

Goodwin, Doris Kearns. *No Ordinary Time: Franklin and Eleanor Roosevelt, the Home Front in World War II.* New York: Simon & Schuster, 1994.

Grant, Julia Dent. *The Personal Memoirs of Julia Dent Grant.* New York: Putnam, 1975.

Grondahl, Paul. *I Rose Like a Rocket: The Political Education of Theodore Roosevelt.* New York: Free Press, 2004.

Hagedorn, Hermann. *The Roosevelt Family of Sagamore Hill.* New York: Macmillan, 1954.

Harris, Bill. *The First Ladies Fact Book: The Childhoods, Courtships, Marriages, Campaigns, Accomplishments, and*

Legacies of Every First Lady from Martha Washington to Michelle Obama. New York: Black Dog & Leventhal, 2009.

Hatch, Alden. *Edith Bolling Wilson: First Lady Extraordinary.* New York: Dodd, Mead, 1961.

Hay, Peter. *All the Presidents' Ladies: Anecdotes of the Women behind the Men in the White House.* New York: Penguin Books, 1988.

Healy, Diana Dixon. *America's First Ladies: Private Lives of the Presidential Wives.* New York: Atheneum, 1988.

Heckscher, August. *Woodrow Wilson: A Biography.* New York: Scribner, 1991.

Helm, Katherine. *The True Story of Mary, Wife of Lincoln.* New York: Harper, 1928.

Herndon, William, and Jesse Weik. *Life of Lincoln.* 1930. Reprint, Cleveland: World Publishing Co., 1943.

Holland, Barbara. *Hail to the Chiefs: How to Tell Your Polks from Your Tylers.* New York: Ballantine Books, 1990.

Hoover, Irvin H. *Forty-Two Years in the White House.* Boston: Houghton Mifflin, 1934.

Irwin, Will. *Herbert Hoover: A Reminiscent Biography.* New York: Grosset & Dunlap, 1928.

James, Marquis. *The Life of Andrew Jackson.* Indianapolis: Bobbs-Merrill, 1938.

Johnson, Willis Fletcher. *The Life of Warren G. Harding: From the Simple Life of the Farm to the Glamor and Power of the White House.* Philadelphia: John C. Winston Co., 1923.

Kelly, C. Brian. *Best Little Stories from the White House.* Nashville: Cumberland House, 1999.

Kohlsaat, H. H. *From McKinley to Harding.* New York: Scribner, 1923.

Korda, Michael. *Ulysses S. Grant: The Unlikely Hero.* New York: HarperCollins, 2004.

Kunhardt, Philip B., Jr., and Philip B. Kunhardt III. *The American President.* New York: Riverhead Books, 1999.

Lash, Joseph P. *Eleanor and Franklin: The Story of Their Relationship.* New York: Norton, 1971.

———. *Eleanor Roosevelt: A Friend's Memoir.* Garden City, NY: Doubleday, 1964.

Lathem, Edward Connery, ed. *Meet Calvin Coolidge: The Man behind the Myth.* Brattleboro, VT: Stephen Greene Press, 1960.

Levin, Phyllis Lee. *Abigail Adams: A Biography.* New York: St. Martin's Press, 1987.

Lewis, Lloyd. *Captain Sam Grant.* Boston: Little, Brown & Co., 1950.

Link, Arthur. *Woodrow Wilson: A Brief Biography.* Cleveland: World Publishing Co., 1963.

Lippman, Theodore, Jr. *The Squire of Warm Springs: F.D.R. in Georgia.* Chicago: Playboy Press, 1977.

Logan, Mrs. John A. *Thirty Years in Washington.* Hartford, CT: Worthington & Co., 1901.

Longworth, Alice Roosevelt. *Crowded Hours.* New York: Scribner's, 1933.

Marquis Publications. *Who Was Who in America.* 2 vols. Chicago: Marquis, 1966.

Marszalek, John F. *The Petticoat Affair: Manners, Mutiny, and Sex in Andrew Jackson's White House.* New York: Free Press, 1997.

Mayer, Dale C. *Lou Henry Hoover: A Prototype for First Ladies.* New York: Nova History Publications, 2004.

McAdoo, Eleanor Wilson. *The Priceless Gift: The Love Letters of Woodrow Wilson and Ellen Axson Wilson.* New York: McGraw-Hill, 1962.

———, and Gaffey, Margaret. *The Woodrow Wilsons.* New York: Macmillan, 1937.

McCullough, David. *Truman.* New York: Simon & Schuster, 1992.

McFeely, William S. *Grant: A Biography.* New York: Norton, 1981.

Means, Marianne. *The Woman in the White House: The Life, Times and Influence of Twelve Notable First Ladies.* New York: Random House, 1963.

Mee, Charles L., Jr. *The Ohio Gang: The World of Warren G. Harding.* New York: M. Evans, 1981.

Moore, Virginia. *The Madisons: A Biography*. New York: McGraw-Hill, 1979.

Morris, Edmund. *The Rise of Theodore Roosevelt*. New York: Coward, McCann & Geoghegan, 1979.

———. *Theodore Rex*. New York: Random House, 2001.

Morris, Sylvia Jukes. *Edith Kermit Roosevelt: Portrait of a First Lady*. New York: Coward, McCann & Geoghegan, 1980.

Moses, John B., and Wilbur Cross. *Presidential Courage*. New York: Norton, 1980.

Nagel, Paul C. *The Adams Women: Abigail and Louisa Adams, Their Sisters and Daughters*. New York: Oxford University Press, 1987.

———. *Descent from Glory: Four Generations of the John Adams Family*. New York: Oxford University Press, 1983.

———. *John Quincy Adams: A Public Life, a Private Life*. New York: Knopf, 1997.

Nichols, Roy F. *Young Hickory of the Granite Hills*. 2nd ed. Philadelphia: University of Pennsylvania Press, 1958.

Nolan, Jeanette Covert. *Dolley Madison*. New York: Messner, 1958.

O'Toole, Patricia. *When Trumpets Call: Theodore Roosevelt after the White House*. New York: Simon & Schuster, 2005.

Peare, Catherine Owens. *The Herbert Hoover Story*. New York: Crowell, 1965.

————. *The Woodrow Wilson Story.* New York: Crowell, 1963.

Pryor, Helen B. *Lou Henry Hoover: Gallant First Lady.* New York: Dodd, Mead, 1969.

Randall, Willard Sterne. *George Washington: A Life.* New York: Henry Holt, 1997.

Richards, Leonard L. *The Life and Times of Congressman John Quincy Adams.* New York: Oxford University Press, 1986.

Roosevelt, Eleanor. *On My Own.* New York: Harper, 1958.

Roosevelt, Elliott, and James Brough. *Mother R: Eleanor Roosevelt's Untold Story.* New York: Putnam, 1977.

Roosevelt, James. *My Parents: A Differing View.* Chicago: Playboy Press, 1976.

————, and Sidney Shallet. *Affectionately, F. D. R.* New York: Harcourt, Brace, 1959.

Ross, Ishbel. *An American Family: The Tafts.* Cleveland: World Publishing Co., 1964.

————. *The General's Wife: The Life of Mrs. Ulysses S. Grant.* New York: Dodd, Mead, 1959.

————. *Grace Coolidge and Her Era: The Story of a President's Wife.* New York: Dodd, Mead, 1962.

————. *Power with Grace: The Life Story of Mrs. Woodrow Wilson.* New York: Putnam, 1975.

———. *The President's Wife: Mary Todd Lincoln.* New York: Putnam, 1973.

Russell, Francis. *The Shadow of Blooming Grove: Warren G. Harding in His Times.* New York: McGraw-Hill, 1968.

Saunders, Frances Wright. *Ellen Axson Wilson: First Lady Between Two Worlds.* Chapel Hill: University of North Carolina Press, 1985.

Schachtman, Tom. *Edith and Woodrow: A Presidential Romance.* New York: Putnam, 1981.

Seager, Robert, III. *And Tyler Too.* New York: McGraw-Hill, 1963.

Seale, William. *The President's House: A History.* 2 vols. Washington, DC: White House Historical Association, 1986.

Shepherd, Jack. *The Adams Chronicles: Four Generations of Greatness.* Boston: Little, Brown & Co., 1975.

———. *Cannibals of the Heart: A Personal Biography of Louisa Catherine and John Quincy Adams.* New York: McGraw-Hill, 1980.

Sievers, Harry J. *Benjamin Harrison.* 3 vols. Chicago: Regnery, 1952–58.

Sinclair, Andrew. *The Available Man: The Life behind the Masks of Warren Gamaliel Harding.* New York: Macmillan, 1965.

Smith, Gene. *The Shattered Dream: Herbert Hoover and the Great Depression.* New York: Morrow, 1970.

————. *When the Cheering Stopped: The Last Years of Woodrow Wilson.* New York: Morrow, 1964.

Smith, Marie, and Louise Durbin. *White House Brides.* Washington, DC: Acropolis Books, 1966.

Stoddard, Henry L. *As I Knew Them: Presidents and Politics from Grant to Coolidge.* New York: Harper & Brothers, 1927.

Sullivan, Mark. *Our Times.* Vol. 5, *Over Here, 1914–1918.* New York: Scribner, 1933.

Sullivan, Michael John. *Presidential Passions: The Love Affairs of America's Presidents—From Washington and Jefferson to Kennedy and Johnson.* New York: Shapolsky Publishers, 1991.

Taft, Helen Herron. *Recollections of Full Years.* New York: Dodd, Mead, 1914.

Thompson, Charles Willis. *Presidents I've Known and Two Near Presidents.* Indianapolis: Bobbs-Merrill, 1929.

Todd, Helen. *A Man Named Grant.* Boston: Houghton Mifflin, 1940.

Tribble, Edwin, ed. *A President in Love: The Courtship Letters of Woodrow Wilson and Edith Bolling Galt.* Boston: Houghton Mifflin, 1981.

Truman, Margaret. *Bess W. Truman.* New York: Macmillan, 1986.

————. *First Ladies.* New York: Random House, 1995.

———. *Harry S. Truman.* New York: Morrow, 1973.

———. *Letters from Father: The Truman Family's Personal Correspondence.* New York: Arbor House, 1981.

———. *Where the Buck Stops: The Personal and Private Writings of Harry S. Truman.* New York: Warner, 1969.

Tumulty, Joseph P. *Woodrow Wilson as I Know Him.* Garden City, NY: Doubleday, Page and Co., 1921.

Wead, Doug. *All the President's Children: Triumph and Tragedy in the Lives of America's First Families.* New York: Atria Books, 2003.

Weinstein, Edwin A. *Woodrow Wilson: A Medical and Psychological Biography.* Princeton, NJ: Princeton University Press, 1981.

White, William Allen. *A Puritan in Babylon: The Story of Calvin Coolidge.* New York: Macmillan, 1938.

Whitney, Janet. *Abigail Adams.* Boston: Little, Brown & Co., 1947.

Wikander, Lawrence E., and Robert H. Ferrell, eds. *Grace Coolidge: An Autobiography.* Worland, WY: High Plains Publishing, 1992.

Wilentz, Sean. *Andrew Jackson.* New York: Times Books, 2005.

Wilson, Edith Bolling. *My Memoir.* Indianapolis: Bobbs-Merrill, 1939.

Withey, Lynne. *Dearest Friend: A Life of Abigail Adams.* New York: Free Press, 1981.

Woodward, William E. *Meet General Grant.* New York: Horace Liveright, 1928.

ABOUT THE AUTHOR

Feather Schwartz Foster has been an independent presidential historian for more than three decades, with a personal library of more than twelve hundred president-related volumes.

After spending thirty-five years in advertising and public relations with various agencies and industrial firms, she now lectures about the "old" First Ladies at adult education venues associated with the College of William and Mary and Christopher Newport University. *The First Ladies* is her fourth book.

She lives in Williamsburg, Virginia.